WILL WILL AND ME
Eight Amazing Stories About Two Special Friends

WILL WILL AND ME

EIGHT AMAZING STORIES ABOUT TWO SPECIAL FRIENDS

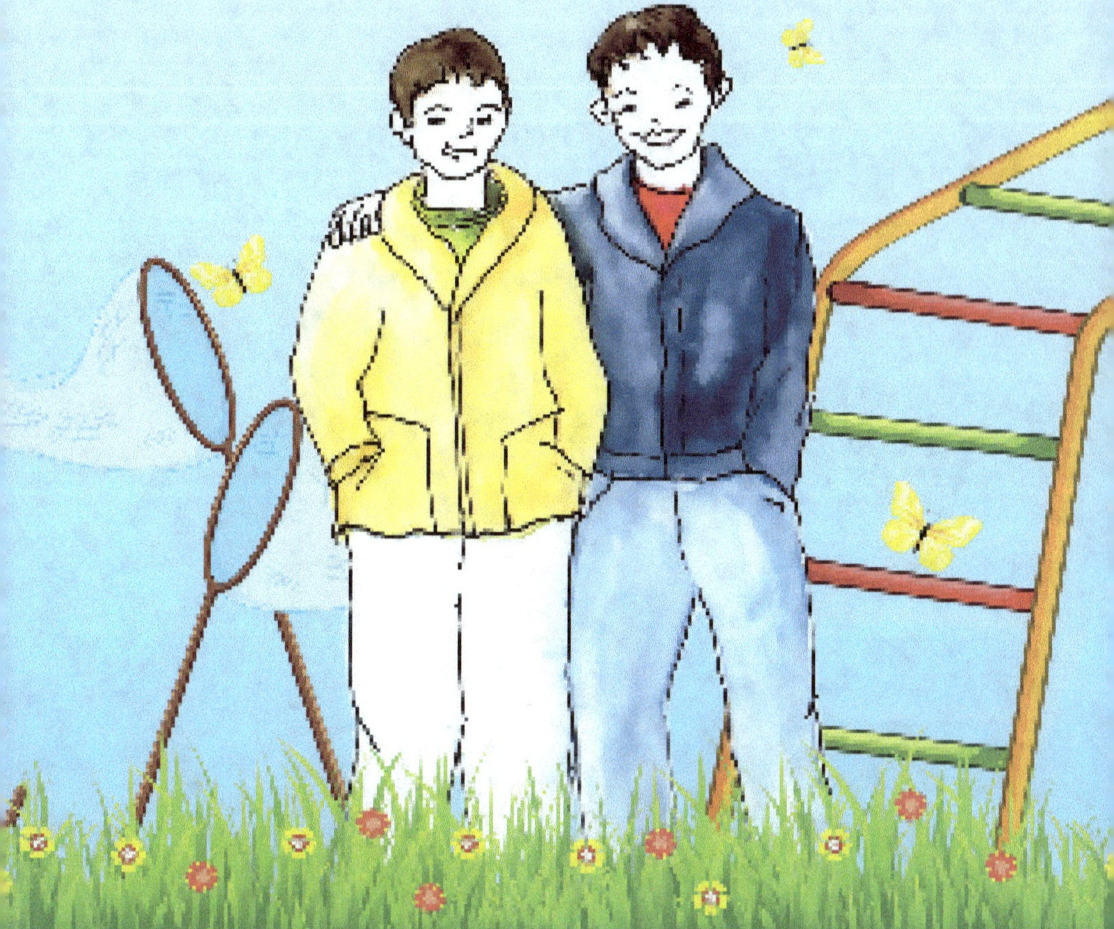

JOHN HYLAND
PICTURES BY ELDORA LARSON

Copyright @2020 by (John Hyland)

All rights reserved. No part of this book may be reproduced in any form or by any electronic or mechanical means, including information storage and retrieval systems, without permission in writing from the publisher, except by reviewers, who may quote brief passages in a review.

This publication contains the opinions and ideas of its author. It is intended to provide helpful and informative material on the subjects addressed in the publication. The author and publisher specifically disclaim all responsibility for any liability, loss or risk, personal or otherwise, which is incurred as a consequence, directly or indirectly, of the use and application of any of the contents of this book.

WORKBOOK PRESS LLC
187 E Warm Springs Rd,
Suite B285, Las Vegas, NV 89119, USA

Website: https://workbookpress.com/
Hotline: 1-888-818-4856
Email: admin@workbookpress.com

Ordering Information:
Quantity sales. Special discounts are available on quantity purchases by corporations, associations, and others. For details, contact the publisher at the address above.

Library of Congress Control Number: 2016949796
ISBN-13:   978-1-952754-12-8 (Paperback Version)
                              978-1-952754-96-8 (Digital Version)

REV. DATE: (03/09/2020)

Contents

One: How Will Will Got His Name	2
Two: Butterfly Collecting Can Be Dangerous	6
Three: Yankees and Confederates	13
Four: Beware of Hairpins and Rubber Bands	22
Five: Will Will's Fun Place	29
Six: Will Will Helps Out — Really!	40
Seven: Snagging Mr. Whiskers	48
Eight: A Perfect Job?	57

ONE:
HOW WILL WILL GOT HIS NAME

Some people would have to stop and think if you asked them to name the best friend they've ever had. But not me. I'd tell you right away that special person was my grade-school pal, Will Will.

You'd probably give me a funny look and ask if I was joking, or wonder why I repeated words when I didn't have to. I'd say I was perfectly serious because my best friend's name really was Will Will — with two Wills. I've got to admit he hadn't always been Will Will. Like a caterpillar before it becomes a butterfly, he'd been born William Sidney Peterson in a town in northern Illinois where both of us grew up in the 1950s and '60s.

His fancy birthday name might have been OK if Will Will had been a guy who stayed indoors and acted snooty. Instead, he loved to play dodge ball, catch frogs and snakes, and do everything else your average red-blooded kid enjoys. He was just one of the guys to me and the rest of his friends, so we just called him Will before he became Will Will.

Unfortunately, his grandma always used his caterpillar-before-butterfly name. "Why, William Sidney! What a handsome young man you're getting to be!" she'd tell him. That was an exaggeration because Will Will was just a kid, with puffy cheeks, a broad nose, and a small mouth. His brown eyes were narrow but always moving. He seemed to be looking every which way at the same time.

The rest of Will Will's body was always moving, too. He couldn't sit or stand still because things around him lured him into action. Whenever a butterfly fluttered into his yard, he couldn't resist grabbing a net and chasing it. If the thought of making an underground fort popped into his head, he'd pick up a shovel and start digging almost anywhere.

Because Will Will used up so much energy, he was quite thin. His T-shirts and blue jeans hung loosely on his chest, arms and legs. His shoes were just right, however. They were high-topped gym sneakers that gave him perfect traction whenever he dashed into foolish situations.

Will Will had brains, but he didn't use them right. The intelligence that should have gone into school work got detoured into mischief. That upset his mom, who said he was a "scalawag." His older brother Dan made fun of his bad grades by calling him "Willy Lump Lump" after a thick-headed character played by the famous comedian Red Skelton.

"But how did he become Will Will?" you're probably asking. "Didn't you say he used to be just Will to all of his friends?" He was — until we were in fourth grade. Then something strange happened. A bunch of us guys were playing tag in Will's back yard when I heard his little sister Polly singing "Will, Will, Will, Will, Will, he's dumb but pretty nice" to the tune of "Row, row, row your boat, gently down the stream." That was silly, of course, but Polly had a habit of making up dumb songs, so I didn't think anything of it.

Part of the song must have stuck in my brain, however, because the next day during school recess I caught myself yelling, "Hey Will Will! I'll race you to the jungle bars!" As soon as I spoke, guys playing around me gave me funny looks.

"Why did you call Will 'Will Will'?" asked Nick Flanagan. "I'd never do that!"

"Yeah, that was stupid!" yelled Ralphie Monson, who liked to make fun of everybody.

"Cut it out!" I shouted. "My tongue just got twisted a little, and you guys are making a big deal out of it!"

Ralphie wanted me to look really foolish, so he opened his huge mouth, exposed his crooked teeth, and shouted, "Hey, Will, Johnny just gave you a dumb new name! He called you 'Will Will'. What d'ya think of that?"

Ralphie expected Will to agree that the name was stupid, but he smiled and said, "It's not bad at all. I've been called a lot worse."

All of us admired Will for being so full of energy and for doing so many funny things. So whenever he said he liked something, most of us agreed with him.

"Will Will's a great name," Bobby Mason shouted as soon as he heard Will answer Ralphie. "It's just right for him."

Now Ralphie looked foolish, but he wasn't ready to admit he'd been wrong. "Oh yeah?" he yelled at Bobby. "What's so great about 'Will Will'?"

Bobby thought for a few seconds, then said, "It's a special name. No other

kid in our school has it. And Will's a special guy. Nobody else can climb up and down the jungle bars five times without stopping. And remember how he used his fish pole to fly that great big orange kite? It was really funny when those cans he'd tied on its tail kept going clank, clank, clank!"

Bobby's words won us over. Our new Will Will really was special, but not just because he had so much pep and did so many zany things. He was also head-and-shoulders above everyone else at getting himself — and me — into crazy situations, as you'll soon find out.

TWO:
Butterfly Collecting Can Be Dangerous

Most of the crazy stuff that happened to Will Will and me sort of snuck up on us. We'd start out doing the kinds of things any kids might do to have fun. But before we knew it, some of Will Will's wild ideas would get us into trouble.

Like the time in fourth grade when we started collecting butterflies without knowing we'd catch something a lot bigger and a lot harder to handle.

It all began when Will Will and I found an interesting book called *The Beginner's Guide to Butterfly Collecting*. The man who wrote it used a lot of big words. However, he said we could catch lots of butterflies with just a few simple pieces of equipment we could make ourselves. He even put in a lot of pictures so we wouldn't get confused.

The writer said we should make nets first. He explained that we had to have heavy wires for the hoops and cloth for the net parts. Then we'd need wooden poles for the handles. We were supposed to bend the wires around the top of a pail to shape the hoops. Then we'd sew the cloth onto the hoops. We'd finish by attaching the hoops to the handles by using a hammer and metal staples.

Most of this stuff was easy to get. The wire and staples came from Fairfax's hardware store, and Mom gave us the cloth and a needle and thread. Dad loaned us his hammer — after he made us promise not to lose it. Then we sawed the handles off a couple of old brooms we'd found at Will Will's grandma's house.

We had trouble finding the pail, though. It had to be made of sturdy wood or metal so we'd be able to bend the wires around it into perfect circles. The pail also had to be a foot wide. *The Beginner's Guide* didn't say if it could be a little smaller or larger, so we thought it had to be a perfect twelve-incher. Since pails were everywhere, we thought it would be easy to find the right one.

Four turned up in Will Will's garage. None was the exact width, so we rummaged through my garage. In a few minutes the whole floor was covered with rakes, lawn chairs, garden hoses, and lots of other stuff thrown every which way. When I looked up at the ceiling, I spotted a rusty bucket on a sheet of plywood laid across the rafters.

I elbowed Will Will to get his attention. "I'll bet that's the right pail," I declared. "Help me set up this step ladder and I'll get it down."

As Will Will steadied the ladder, I began climbing. The ladder wasn't very high; so when I got to the top step, I had to reach way above my head for the pail. As I pulled it toward me, I could tell there was something in it.

"Be ready to grab this sucker when I hand it down," I told Will Will. "Right-oh!" he sang out. "Just don't drop it on my noggin."

I didn't drop the pail, but whatever was in it made it lopsided, and my hand slipped on the top. It tipped down, spilling a whole mess of dry, dusty grass seed. Will Will got a face full, but most of it went down the front and back of his shirt. Some even worked its way into his blue jeans and underpants.

"Cryminny!" he sputtered. "How could you be such a moron, Johnny? This stuff itches and tastes crappy!"

I scrambled down the ladder, apologizing like mad. "Jeez, Will Will, I'm really sorry! It's all my fault. But at least the pail didn't fall and conk you."

Will Will didn't answer because he was too busy spitting out seed. Next, he peeled off his shirt and jeans and shorts and gave them a good shaking. I shouldn't have laughed, but it isn't every day you see a kid standing bare naked in a garage, scratching himself with one hand and swinging his clothes around his head with the other.

"You say one word about this to other guys and I'll pound you!" Will Will shouted.

After he calmed down and put his clothes back on, we measured the pail. It was thirteen inches across. We would have continued searching for a twelve-incher, but we didn't know where else to look. We just gave up and started bending the wire out on the lawn.

The bending wasn't easy because the pail moved every time we tried to shape the hoop around it. Then Will Will had a bright idea. "One of us has to stand in the bucket to hold it down while the other guy works on the wire."

Naturally he expected me to supply the weight, since he'd just furnished the brains. But as soon as I got both feet in the pail, I lost my balance and fell flat on my back.

As I rolled around gasping for breath, Will Will calmly rubbed his chin and said, "Hmmm. We've got a problem, Johnny. If you keel over again, you'll probably knock the pail cattywumpus. We've gotta move it to the other side of the sidewalk so you can hold on to your little brother's swing set while you're in the pail."

"What if Sammy comes out and wants to swing?" I wheezed.

"You worry about the dumbest things, Johnny! Just get back in the pail so I can get going on the hoops."

After the hoops were finished, everything else went fast. However, I bashed my fingers as I pounded the staples into the handles to attach the hoops. That was because Will Will was yacking at me for hammering the staples in crooked — although they never came loose.

The last thing we did was make butterfly-collecting containers by putting cotton dipped in rubbing alcohol into a couple of empty mayonnaise jars.

As soon as all our equipment was ready, we started hunting butterflies. We didn't have to go far because we lived on the edge of town near lots of woods and fields. We knew just what to look for because we'd read a chapter in *The Beginner's Guide* called "Butterflies of the Midwest."

We'd only walked a few yards down a dirt road when we came to a big puddle. Clouds of small white cabbage butterflies and yellow sulfurs were flitting up and down above the muddy water. They looked like they wanted to dive in. Their reflections made it seem like just as many butterflies had already made the plunge and were hogging all the space in the puddle.

That crazy thought had just popped into my head when Will Will hollered, "Let's catch a bunch of these little guys to make sure our nets work! Then if we run into monarchs and swallowtails and painted ladies, we'll be all warmed up."

We started swinging our nets. With each swoop we netted four or five of the above-puddle butterflies, making the under-water ones vanish. Soon our collecting jars were half full.

It was time to hunt larger butterflies, so we started tramping through a field full of tall grass and wildflowers. A light wind swayed the grass stems and fluttered their tops, which looked like long, thin birds' toes. Bright yellow sunflowers with brown centers nodded like they were glad to see us, even though we might trample them if we didn't watch where we were going.

There were also lots of milkweeds. *The Beginner's Guide* said they attracted monarchs, so I wanted to see if anything was fluttering among those plants. I saw large oval leaves and seed pods shaped like small hairy footballs with pointed ends. I also noticed clusters of pinkish-purple flowers — but no butterflies.

"Hey, Johnny!" yelled Will Will. "Quit gawking at those weeds and look straight ahead."

That was an insult, but it was just in time to make me notice two monarchs flying a few yards in front of us. They were floating along on their black-lined orange wings. Then when we started chasing them, they zig-zagged as fast as we could run. It took a ton of energy and lots of net swoops before we caught them. As I pulled my monarch from my net, I was surprised to see that its thin body was coal black with white dots.

"Now we're getting somewhere," Will Will panted. "I hope we can snag some other butterflies that are just as great as these guys!"

Our snagging went fine because we caught two more monarchs, five red admirals, and even a giant swallowtail in only half an hour.

"OK, Will Will," I said. "Let's go home and pin up our butterflies. Remember what the book told us about spreading their wings out before they get too dry?"

Will Will had a mischievous smile. "Let's wait a while. I've just figured out a neat new way to use our nets. We'll try them out on Old Man Beatty's geese."

Old Man Beatty had a small farm about a quarter of a mile down the road. He grew corn and soy beans and kept a few pigs and beef cattle. But he spent most of his time raising about a hundred chickens, ducks and geese. He gave a lot of them pet names and let them wander around wherever they wanted to go.

None of those birds went far because Old Man Beatty fed them all the time. They just hung around the front yard of his ramshackle house and wandered out into the road. Cars had to slow way down to keep from hitting them, and anyone walking past had to put up with the geese. They'd waddle right up to you, stretch their long necks high in the air, and go "HONK! HONK!" And if they were feeling ornery when they saw you, they'd flap their wings and give your legs a good nip.

"We'd better not monkey with the geese," I warned Will Will. "If we hurt any of them, Old Man Beatty might kick our butts. Besides, some of those long-necked guys are bigger than our nets and pretty dangerous."

"We've got nothing to worry about," Will Will insisted. "Old Man Beatty's too fat and gimpy to chase us, and we'll only catch a couple of the small geese. Besides, we'll let them go right away."

I told Will Will I thought that was a bad idea, but he was already loping down the road toward Old Man Beatty's farm. "Aw, what the heck," I said as I hurried after him.

The geese were waiting. In fact, they came half running and half flying up the road to meet us. The first one that got close was a huge gray gander, hissing with a half-opened bill. It looked like it wanted to peck us to pieces.

I don't know if Will Will was trying to protect himself or just having fun, but he slammed his net down hard over the monster. The goose was so big that the net covered only half its body, but its wings got caught up inside the hoop. The next second it was thrashing around on its side in the road, honking like crazy. It twisted the hoop six ways to Saturday but couldn't tear through the cloth.

"Let's get out of here!" I shouted.

"Not 'til I get my net back!" yelled Will Will, bracing his feet and holding on to the handle with both hands.

Just then I saw Old Man Beatty running up the road toward us. His flabby stomach was bouncing above his short, churning legs. His face was beet red, and he was shaking his fist. As he barreled toward us, his big-brim hat flew off the back of his head.

"Drop that stupid net and take off!" I yelled. Will Will yanked hard on the handle, and suddenly the net tore wide open. The goose got to its feet, flopped off the road, and disappeared into a clump of bushes. All of the other birds on the road were flopping around, too, trying to get out of Old Man Beatty's way.

He was only a few yards from us when we started to run, and we could hear him huffing and puffing at our heels. We probably would have escaped if we hadn't been lugging our nets. They slowed us down just enough so Old Man Beatty was able to grab our shoulders and spin us around.

Before we knew what was happening, he had two fist-fulls of our shirts. We could feel his damp wheezy breath against our faces and smell the stink of manure from his clothes.

"I should give your kids a good licking right now," he panted. "But I'm gonna

let you tell me why you were messing with my geese. You were out catching butterflies and just couldn't pass up the chance to snag a really big one — right?"

Old Man Beatty was smiling, so I could see he wasn't too mad. I don't know for sure, but I think he was planning to let us go because he remembered some goofy trick he pulled when he was a kid himself.

Will Will ruined everything. He was the kind of guy who'd tell ridiculous stretchers to try to get out of trouble, and that riled a lot of people.

"No, sir, Mr. Beatty!" he exclaimed. "We weren't trying to snag your geese. That big dumb gray bozo just ran into my net while me and Johnny were walking down the road."

The smile disappeared from Old Man Beatty's face, and he tightened his grip on our shirts. "You're lying, you little snot!" he shouted. "I was watching from my front yard and saw you slam that net down on poor old Jack. You're sure gonna wish you'd 'fessed up!"

You can probably guess what happened next. Old Man Beatty turned Will Will bottom up and gave him a good hiding. Then he tanned my britches, just for "general principles," he said. When he was finished, he told us we'd get a double dose of the same thing if he ever caught us around his farm again.

As we limped home we were crying, but Will Will said our run-in with Old Man Beatty hadn't been so bad. "I'll bet that dumb jerk's got a sore hand from pounding on us," he sniffed. "And if he hadn't been spying on us, he'd have swallowed my story!"

"And if you hadn't told that stupid fib, he wouldn't have blistered us! Dang it, Will Will! When're you gonna learn you can't lie all the time?"

"I don't lie! I just stretch things once in a while to have a little fun."

What more could I say? Will Will wouldn't listen to reason, so I clammed up and kept walking. But I made up my mind not to let him get me into trouble again. Of course he did, but that's another story.

THREE:
Yankees and Confederates

As I've already said, Will Will didn't do well in school. He had no interest in regular subjects like arithmetic, social studies or reading, and he never learned much when our teachers came up with special projects. So you can imagine how he acted when our fifth-grade teacher, Mrs. Westfall, told us we were going to study the Civil War.

Normally we wouldn't have had to do that, but it was 1961, and lots of people were excited about the centennial of the war. Wherever you looked in newspapers and magazines, you saw pictures of Abe Lincoln, Jeff Davis, General Grant and General Lee. Even Newberry's dime store downtown got into the act by selling Yankee and Confederate caps.

Our school seemed like the right place to learn about the war because it looked about a hundred years old. It was a huge two-story building on a rough-cut limestone foundation. Its walls were made of brown weathered bricks, and it had long rows of windows with white wooden sills and frames. It also had a steep, shingled roof with a brick chimney at each end.

If you looked at the front of the school, you'd see a huge castle-like tower with a white cement surface and four big windows near the top. And at the bottom you'd notice the school's main entrance. It had a glass-paned door, and on both sides were American flags carved in stone.

I didn't really know if the school was as old as the Civil War, but I was sure Mrs. Westfall would feel right at home as she told us about Yankees and Confederates.

But Will Will didn't think so.

"I don't want to listen to Mrs. Westfall!" he complained. "She's gonna talk about a bunch of guys who had beards, wore old-fashioned clothes, hated each other, and are all dead now."

"You might change your mind if you listen to her," I replied. "Just sit at your desk and pay attention."

"The heck with that! I might be in my seat, but I won't hear a thing she says!"

Will Will did his best to ignore Mrs. Westfall. When she told us how the

Southern States had started the war by trying to set up their own country, he slouched at his desk and scraped the paint off two pencils with a nail file. Then he bit the erasures off the pencils and stuck them into his ears when she explained how the North fought the South to keep the United States from breaking up.

I didn't think Mrs. Westfall had any chance of getting through to Will Will. Then all of a sudden she held up a big colored picture that caught his eye. It showed about ten thousand Yankees and Confederates dressed in blue and gray uniforms running around shooting at each other.

When Will Will saw the picture, he sat up straight and pulled the erasures out of his ears. He listened carefully while Mrs. Westfall explained that it was a painting of the Battle of Gettysburg. As soon as she finished, his hand shot up into the air.

Mrs. Westfall was shocked because this was the first time Will Will had shown much interest in the subjects she taught. "M-m-my goodness William," she stammered, hardly believing what she saw. "Do you have something to say?"

"Can you please tell us more about the fights the Yankees and Confederates got into?" he asked politely.

Mrs. Westfall said she'd be glad to give him more information about Civil War battles tomorrow, as soon as she had a chance to look it up. I'm sure she knew everything already but needed time to get over her shock. She was happy, however, and praised Will Will for wanting to learn.

Most of us kids **weren't** happy – as Will Will found out during recess on the playground.

"Hey, Will Will!" shouted Ralphie Monson from the top of the jungle bars. "Why were you buttering up Mrs. Westfall? Looks like you were trying to be teacher's pet!"

Teddy Robbins, who was teeter-totterring with Davy Schuster, yelled, "You'd better be careful, old buddy, or you'll be a real apple polisher!"

All the rest of us were standing around wondering what Will Will would say. We hated to think he was trying to get in good with Mrs. Westfall to show us up, but that's what it looked like.

"You guys are real flea brains!" he snorted. "Here I am, working on a really neat game called 'Yankees and Confederates,' and you say I'm a butter-up guy!"

Will Will knew how well we enjoyed the fun things he invented, so he stopped for about five seconds to let what he'd just said sink into our brains. Then he hit us where it hurt.

"Of course, if nobody wants to play 'Yankees and Confederates,' I'll forget all about it."

Like magic, everyone started slapping him on the back and telling him they'd known all along he had a good reason for getting interested in the Civil War.

Ralphie and Teddy were especially friendly. "Ask Mrs. Westfall anything you want!" they begged. "Just make sure 'Yankees and Confederates' is a super game!"

The next morning Mrs. Westfall gave Will Will all the information he needed about Civil War battles. She said huge armies of Yankees and Confederates would march all around, camping each night and sizing each other up. Then when their generals told them to, they'd pitch into each other with muskets, swords and cannons until one army gave up and retreated.

The army that won would take lots of prisoners, then get ready for the next battle.

By afternoon recess, Will Will had the whole game figured out. All of us crowded around to hear what we were going to do. "Everybody'll pretend to be a Yankee or Confederate, and we'll have our own Civil War right here on the playground!" he announced.

"Are we gonna use guns and swords and cannons?" asked Ben Fredericks.

"Of course not, you dope! Somebody could get hurt, and where do you suppose we'd get them?"

Since no one wanted to ask any more stupid questions, Will Will continued his explanation.

"We'll wear Yankee and Confederate caps so we can tell each other apart. We can buy them at Newberry's dime store right after school today and be ready to start the game tomorrow. We'll run around during morning recess and grab each others' caps. The guys whose caps get snatched will be prisoners 'til the bell rings. Then we'll start the game all over again in the afternoon."

Will Will said each side would have a "general" and a "camp" where the prisoners would be kept. Everybody had to do exactly what their generals told them, or they'd get kicked out of the game.

After all of us agreed to follow the rules, Will Will said he should be one of the generals because he'd invented "Yankees and Confederates." He also said his side should be the Confederates because gray was his favorite color.

No one griped about that, but there was trouble when both Mike Reynolds and Teddy Robbins wanted to be the Yankee general. They started to argue, but Will Will settled things by flipping a coin. Mike won, which upset Teddy, but he had no reason to complain.

Now the only thing left to do was choose sides. There were twelve of us, so each side would have six guys on it. Will Will and Mike said they'd pick whoever they wanted, but they had to decide who should go first.

The coin spun into the air again, and Mike got the first choice. He took big-mouth Ralphie, and Will Will took me. In about two minutes, everybody else was picked.

"Yankees and Confederates" was a lot of fun, as you can imagine, but it got pretty rough. Whenever a kid got his cap snatched, he was supposed to give up right away and become a prisoner. Often he got mad and started swinging, and about four guys wound up with fat lips.

At first Will Will thought this was no problem because our Confederates took most of the prisoners. We'd all roam around together until we saw one or two Yankees by themselves. In a flash, a couple of us would grab their caps. The rest of us would drag them to our prison camp, which was under a huge maple tree in back of the school.

We didn't do so well when the Yankees started sticking together, too. As soon as they saw us, Mike the general would yell "charge!" and they'd all attack. Then everyone on both sides would push, shove, and try to whip each others' caps off.

Our side usually got the worst of these tussles because the Yankees played dirty tricks. Ralphie dashed up to me one morning and pretended to reach for my cap. As I tried to step back, he kicked my feet out from under me. The next instant I was flat on the ground with nothing on my head. All I could see were Ralphie's wide grinning mouth and ragged teeth a few feet above my face.

"We've got to show those Yankees they're not so hot!" growled Will Will

after he'd been taken prisoner two recesses in a row.

"Well, we could get some sixth graders to help us beat them to a pulp, but then things might really get rough," I replied.

"I've got a better idea," said Will Will. "We'll booby-trap Mike and his Yankees right here on the playground! We'll need a long rope and long nails, a hammer, a thick paper bag, and something sloppy and stinky – like rotten apples."

When I asked how the trap would work, Will Will said he'd show me when we put it together. He said it was complicated but thought we could set it up right after school that day.

As soon as school was out, we went over to Will Will's house and got the rope, hammer, nails, and a big thick paper bag. Then we scooped up a big pail of rotten apples from under the trees in an abandoned orchard, about a half mile down the road from my house.

But just as we were ready to head back to the school yard, we realized we'd have trouble hauling all the stuff. We lived about a mile and a half out in the country and rode our bikes back and forth a lot of the time. However, we didn't think we could carry everything that way. I would have asked Mom to drive us to the playground, but she'd have a fit about the rotten apples.

"Dang it all!" growled Will Will. "We've gotta do some thinking, and that'll take time. We won't be able to booby-trap the Yankees right away."

"Well, tomorrow's Friday," I said. "We should be able to get all our stuff to the playground by Saturday. Can't the trap be ready by Monday?"

"Sure it can," snapped Will Will. "But I was hoping we could get back at the Yankees tomorrow morning. They've snatched our caps so many times they think they own them!"

I knew how Will Will felt, but there wasn't much we could do but try to hold our own the next day. Our six Confederates did put up a pretty good fight, even though two of us wound up prisoners.

When Saturday came, Will Will and I figured out how to use our bikes to get all the things for the Yankee trap to the playground. He carried the rope, hammer, nails and the folded-up bag in a back pack as he rode. I pulled the pail of apples in my little brother's wagon behind my bike.

It took an hour to get to the school because we were on a rough gravel road that made the wagon rattle and bounce most of the way. The pail bounced, too, causing the sloppy apples to churn up and down. I had to pedal real slow so they wouldn't slosh over the top of the pail. That was bad enough because I was hardly going fast enough to keep my balance on my bike. To make matters worse, Will Will laughed as I wobbled from side to side.

When we finally got to the school, we set everything on the ground in our camp beneath the big maple tree. I was bushed from fighting the road and the gravel, but Will Will didn't feel sorry for me. Instead, he started bossing me around.

"Start by pounding one of those long nails half way into the tree trunk right here," he ordered, pointing to a spot about ten inches up from the ground. I felt like complaining, but I zipped my lip so we could get started right away on the booby trap. But I felt more feisty when Will Will expected me to work at top speed.

"Hurry and bend that nail over so it makes a loop," he spouted. "Now put a second one way up there into the trunk, just under that big branch that sticks straight out. And be sure to bend it into a loop, too."

I had to stand on my tip toes to reach the spot where the second nail was supposed to go. Then after I'd hammered it in and was about to bend it over, Will Will said to pull it out and move it an inch lower.

That was the last straw. "Why don't you do it yourself if it's got to be so perfect?" I yelled. "Do you think that we're really Confederates and that I'm a slave who has to do all your work?"

Will Will looked shocked. "Don't you want the trap to work right?" he asked, ignoring my insult and trying to look innocent.

"Sure I do, but I'm not gonna let you stand around doing nothing. You aren't afraid of getting a little dirt on your hands, are you?"

After arguing for about a minute, we took turns doing the rest of the work. Will Will moved and looped the second nail. Then he pounded a third one into the side of the maple's big branch, about four feet out from the trunk. He looped that nail, too, and tied one end of his rope to the bottom of a chain-link fence near the tree. Then he handed the other end to me.

"If it isn't too much trouble, run the rope up through all three nail loops," he said in a wise-acre way. "And unless you think I'm being too bossy, **please** toss the rest of the rope up onto the big branch."

I was all set to say something smart back, but then I realized what he was planning. "Hey!" I exclaimed. "We're gonna set the bag of rotten apples out on the branch and tie the rope to it, aren't we? Then when the Yankees run under the tree and trip the other end, they'll pull the bag down on themselves!"

"Aren't you a genius!" snorted Will Will.

We hurried to finish the trap so we could try it out to make sure it worked right. Instead of using the apples, we put rocks in the bag for practice. Then we tripped the rope and ducked as the bag came whizzing past our heads.

"Super," Will Will shouted. "Our Yankee bopper will clobber them for sure!"

We took the bag and rope down and hid them with the pail of apples in thick bushes next to our camp. We planned to come back early Monday morning and put everything together before school started. Then we'd tell all our Confederates what was going to happen.

Everything was ready when the morning battle started. As soon as we got out on the playground for recess, the Yankees came ripping after us with Mike and Ralphie leading the pack. "Stop and fight!" they yelled. "You can't get away from us!"

We **did** get away by dashing behind the school and into our camp. When we got to the big maple, all of us hopped over the rope and ran about ten yards further. Then we spun around to watch, just as Mike tripped the rope.

Will Will had cut slits in the apple bag to make sure the sloppy stuff would plaster the Yankees as soon as it hit them. That's exactly what happened as the bag bounced off the top of Mike's head and smacked Ralphie square in the face.

All of the other Yankees got clobbered by the rest of the stinky mess as it flew behind Mike and Ralphie. All of them staggered, and a few fell, screaming like they'd been shot by a cannon.

"You guys look terrible and smell awful!" shouted Will Will as we laughed our heads off.

"Oh, yeah?" shouted Mike, as he tried to wipe the sloppy stuff out of his hair. "We'll see who looks and smells bad!"

In a couple of seconds we were rolling on the ground with the Yankees on top of us, trying to keep from getting punched to pieces. Everyone was cussing and grunting and groaning like a bunch of wild men. Now that I think about it, we must've looked like **real** Yankees and Confederates fighting a **real** Civil War battle.

I don't know how long we wrestled and pounded each other, but all of a sudden about four teachers pulled us apart and marched us down to the principal's office. It was hard to tell who was who. All of us had lost our caps and were smeared pretty thick with rotten apples, grass stains and dirt.

To make a long story short, the principal put an end to "Yankees and Confederates." He was really mad to find out that a fifth-grader could make such an awful booby trap. All of us had to stay after school for two days and help the janitors clean blackboards, sweep floors, and empty wastebaskets. And to make matters worse, several of us got our britches tanned when our parents found out what we'd done.

If anyone got off easy, it was Will Will. He'd invented the game and the trap, but his punishment wasn't any worse than what the rest of us got. Even though I wasn't upset, I wondered why the principal hadn't come down harder on him. He thought the trap was terrible, so you'd expect him to lower the boom on the guy who made and used it.

"The prinz changed his mind," Will Will snickered. "All of a sudden he realized how smart I was to invent such a snazzy Yankee stopper. Then he decided to cut me some slack. Now he wishes he had my kind of brains!"

That monstrous malarkey shocked me, even though I was used to hearing his bodacious fibs. Instead of telling him he was crazy, I just shook my head and walked away.

FOUR:
Beware of Hairpins and Rubber Bands

Now that you know about the trouble we got into with Old Man Beatty and about the problems "Yankees and Confederates" caused, you're probably wondering why I went along with Will Will whenever his imagination ran wild. I knew things could go wrong, of course. However, the fun I hoped to have made it worth taking a chance that nothing bad would happen. And sometimes it seemed that we couldn't get into trouble.

Take that Saturday afternoon in the summer when Will Will and I had just finished sixth grade. We had set several empty cans up on my backyard fence and were blowing dry navy beans at them through plastic tubes called pea shooters. We were pretending we were soldiers using machine guns to mow down attacking enemies.

We used our tongues to load the make-believe bullets from our cheeks into the imaginary guns. Then we went "pwuut, pwuut, pwuut" as we fired at the little tin villains before they could charge. Our mouths got sore after we'd blasted them for about fifteen minutes, so we tried to think of a different way to keep defending ourselves.

We sat down on the top step of the back porch and started wracking our brains. A squirrel running up and down a tree disturbed us, so we had to chase it away. Then we went right back to thinking. It got to be a real strain. I was almost ready to give up when the old light bulb blinked on inside my head.

"Let's make slingshots," I said.

"Naw," said Will Will, fiddling with his shoe laces. "We'd have to look for forked tree branches and find an old inner tube to cut up. That would be a lot of work, and the slingshots would be too big to sneak into school."

"Well, maybe we should make smaller ones by using things that are easier to find," I suggested.

Will Will wrinkled his nose the way he always did whenever someone said something he thought was dumb. "Yeah, and maybe we can build a Sherman Tank right here in your backyard!"

I never liked his smart-aleck talk, but he really knew how to zing people.

"Well, why don't you think of something better, Mr. Wise Guy?" I snapped.

"That's just what I'll do! All I need is a little more time."

Both of us kept quiet for about a minute. Then Will Will gave me a friendly whack on the shoulder. "Hey Johnny! I'm sorry I made fun of the little slingshots you were talking about. I think we can make them right now from hairpins and rubber bands and a piece of cloth. We'll need a pair of scissors, too."

I said it was worth a try, so we went into the house and got what we needed. (We made sure Mom didn't see us take her hairpins.) Then we came back out onto the porch and set to work. I should say Will Will set to work because he insisted on making the first slingshot by himself.

"These things may be a lot harder to put together than we think," he announced. "After I've ironed out all the wrinkles, you can help."

"I can do just as good a job as you can right now!" I insisted.

"Maybe, but since I'm the one who invented these babies, I should be the one who starts."

I would have reminded Will Will that the slingshots were my idea in the first place. I didn't want to argue, however, so I just told him to go ahead.

Will Will stuck his tongue out the side of his mouth the way he always did when he was concentrating. Then he bent both sides of a hairpin down so it looked like a small "T." Next, he bent up the two ends of the "T" to make a "U," leaving a little handle at the bottom.

That was the right way to get started, but we couldn't agree on how to continue making our amazing little weapon. Will Will cut two rubber bands open and insisted on tying an end of each one to the top of each side of the "U." That didn't work because the bands slid down the sides when he pulled on them.

"Let me take over," I declared. "I know how to fix that goof-up."

Will Will felt insulted and wouldn't admit that something better could be done. "I'll bet you've got some stupid idea that will screw everything up!" he snarled.

I ignored him and untied the rubber bands. Then I got some thread and wrapped it tightly around the ends of the bands to hold them up where they were supposed to go on the "U." To make sure the bands would never slide down, I knotted the thread several times.

Naturally Will Will was upset because I'd gotten the best of him, but I smoothed things over by saying I trusted him to finish the slingshot. Grabbing the scissors, he cut a pocket from the piece of cloth. Then he poked a hole in each side of the pocket and tied the other ends of the rubber bands through the holes. Now our miniature blaster was ready.

"Let's test this little gem!" said Will Will as he picked up a pebble from the sidewalk.

At first I wondered if the slingshot was too small to be any good. I changed my mind really fast, however, when Will Will plinked me on the ankle below my pants cuff.

"Oww! Watch where you're shooting that thing!" I shouted as I hopped around on one foot. "It feels like a bee just stung me!"

Will Will was too busy looking for another pebble to feel sorry for me. This time he aimed at one of the cans on the fence, which was about ten feet away. The pebble whizzed from the slingshot and hit the can with a "bip." When we looked at it, we saw a little dent in its side.

"What a great invention!" yelled Will Will. "You'd better get busy making one of these gizmos for yourself, Johnny."

As soon as I'd made my own slingshot, we went back to shooting all the cans. We couldn't pepper them as fast as when we blew bean bullets, but our aim was much better. All we had to do was hold the slingshots steady, pull the pockets with the pebbles straight back, and draw a bead on our targets by looking between the two sides of the "U".

With almost every shot, we dinged the cans almost like we were using BB guns.

We were sure the slingshots would work just as well on other targets, so we wandered along the road toward town, wondering what we might find. Soon we came to a house owned by a lady named Mrs. Hensley, who had a pesky short-haired dog named Sparky. He was some kind of sawed-off terrier, so he couldn't really hurt you. However, he'd run out and yap his head off whenever you walked past.

As soon as yappy Sparky saw us, he came tearing out into the road with his mouth and stumpy legs going ninety miles a minute. He was all set to nip at our legs when both of us let fly with our slingshots.

We must have zapped him pretty good because he skidded to a stop in the loose gravel and started yelping. Then he made a bee-line back toward the

house and disappeared behind the garage. We were lucky Mrs. Hensley wasn't around or we'd have been in trouble.

When we got close to town, it was just getting dark, and all of the street lights were winking on. They were the old-fashioned kind with big round bulbs hanging down from flat metal shades about fifteen feet above the ground.

"I'll bet I could zap one of those lights just like that!" bragged Will Will, snapping his fingers.

"Sure you could, but what if someone sees you and calls the cops?"

"Nobody'll spot me if I pop that one just ahead 'cause there's no house near it."

As I watched, Will Will walked up to the light pole and took a shot. His pebble barely missed the bulb and clinked against the shade. He took better aim and fired again. This time the bulb went "thuck" and started to smoke. It stayed on for about three seconds, then flared way up and went out.

I was busy watching the bulb, so I didn't notice that Will Will had disappeared until he whistled softly from behind a tree about ten yards from the pole. When I ran over to see what he wanted, I could tell he was upset.

"We'd better make tracks before the cops come!" he whispered.

"I thought you weren't worried about anyone seeing you."

"I just got to thinking there's probably some kind of alarm that goes off in the electric plant downtown every time somebody busts a light. The people at the plant call the police station, and the cops race out and nab the guys who did it — and that's us!"

I reminded Will Will that he was the one who broke the light, but he said the cops would grab me, too, because I was with him.

I didn't think that would happen, but I let him talk me into hiding in a big patch of weeds about twenty yards back down the road. We stayed there until it was completely dark, slapping mosquitoes and getting all itchy from a bunch of stinging nettles we'd laid in by accident.

When we were sure no cops would show up, we took off for home and decided to be more careful with our slingshots.

We weren't careful, of course, and we got into trouble.

The trouble started when we took our slingshots to the movies the next weekend. We hadn't really planned to use them there, but we'd gotten into the habit of carrying them almost everywhere we went. Both of us just happened to have pebbles in our pockets, too.

When we got bored in the middle of a stupid cowboy picture, we decided to shoot the pebbles way up into the beam of light coming from the movie projector. They lit up like little shooting stars as they sailed through the light beam toward the front of the theater.

We shot the pebbles hard enough so they fell on the stage in front of the screen, where they bounced around for two or three seconds. We couldn't see them land, of course, but we could hear them clicking and skipping. Once in a while a pebble would ping against something made of metal, which was really funny.

As you can imagine, the other people watching the movie wondered what was going on. Before long, some of them got up and started talking to the usher. Then they pointed toward the back of the theater where Will Will and I were. Since we were the only ones sitting there, the usher headed right toward us. We just managed to stuff our slingshots into our pockets before he shined his flashlight into our eyes.

"Come on, you kids!" he ordered in a gruff voice. "We're going to see Mr. Benson."

Old Man Benson was the manager of the theater, and in about two minutes we were standing in front of him in his office. He looked like a fat toad with glasses as he sat behind his desk. As soon as the usher said we'd been throwing things, he scowled. His cheeks and the skin under his chin sagged down almost over his collar, but his lips were drawn back into a tight snarl, showing dull yellow teeth.

"What were you two hooligans throwing?" he asked in a harsh, gravely voice.

Before I could answer, Will Will piped up. "We weren't throwing anything. We were just enjoying that great cowboy picture and thinking about all the other neat movies you show."

Old Man Benson wasn't impressed. "If you weren't throwing, you must have been shooting with that little thingamajig," he growled, pointing to the floor near my foot. I knew we were sunk because there was my slingshot!

Will Will picked it up and looked like he'd never seen it before.

"We don't know nothing about this thingamabob," he answered, as cool as a cucumber. "It's not ours."

"Oh no? Then why did it fall out of your buddy's pocket when you scamps walked into my office?"

Any normal person would've given up and confessed — but not Will Will. As quick as you could wink, he cut loose with one of his ridiculous stretchers.

"Johnny saw the doohickey on the floor by the popcorn machine as we were coming to see you. He picked it up 'cause he thought somebody might trip over it and get hurt. Then he accidentally dropped it when we came into your office."

Of course Old Man Benson didn't swallow that fib. He just got madder and turned the air blue with a lot of words I can't put into this story. His face was beet red. If I hadn't been so scared, I would've laughed at the way his fat cheeks were flopping back and forth.

After he'd calmed down a little, he asked who our parents were. I was afraid Will Will would say we were orphans, or that we'd been raised in the woods by wolves. I decided to tell the truth just to get things over.

Old Man Benson called both of our moms and told them what we'd done. Then he asked them to drive down to the theater and pick us up. "Both of them came, and you can imagine the tongue lashings they gave us. When our moms got us home, they grounded us for a whole week for being so foolish at the theater."

Naturally, Will Will was peeved at me. He said if I had let him do all the talking in Old Man Benson's office, we'd have gotten away without being punished.

I told him Old Man Benson would've killed us for sure if he'd heard one more stupid lie, but that didn't calm Will Will down. He did mellow out in about eight days, though, when he needed someone to hunt tadpoles with him.

"This doesn't mean I'm forgetting how you ratted to Old Man Benson," he growled as we headed for our favorite pond with home-made nets and a couple of empty mayonnaise jars.

"Then why did you ask me to go pollywog hunting if I'm still in your dog house?"

"Why do you think, you jerk? You're my best friend!"

FIVE:
Will Will's Fun Place

When Will Will and I weren't in school, we spent a lot of time at each other's house. I'm not sure why he liked coming over to my house, but I enjoyed his place because I didn't have to be super neat there.

Mom always yelled at me whenever I tracked mud into our kitchen or threw my coat into a corner. But at Will Will's, nobody worried about keeping floors squeaky clean or hanging up clothes all the time. You could walk in and feel right at home.

There were lots of fun things to do at Will Will's place. He had a big back yard where you could play red rover, baseball, or any other game. You could usually catch toads and garter snakes in the weeds behind the garage. Or you could climb up into a huge willow tree and play in a three-level club house that had plywood floors but no walls. If you wondered what his big brother Dan liked to do, you could watch him monkeying with an old junk car in the driveway.

You could also have fun with all the pets. Will Will's big collie, Rex, would fetch sticks and balls and bring you moles he'd dug up. Rex was always friendly around people, but he'd tie right into any stray dog that came by. Then you'd see a big noisy fight.

There were always four or five cats sleeping on the back steps or sitting outside the kitchen door, waiting for someone to pet or feed them. One big white one named Max was a pretty good boxer. He'd swipe and bat at you when you poked him. If you teased him too much, he'd hiss and scratch your fingers.

If you didn't like dogs and cats, you could play with two parakeets named Pete and Repeat, who belonged to Will Will's little sister, Polly. They lived in a cage in the living room, but most of the time they were out, flying all over the house. If you were sitting or standing still, they might land on your shoulder and chirp and squawk in your ear.

These birds could talk, too. Will Will taught them to say things like "Holy Moley" and "Go, Go, White Sox," but they also learned words on their own. Once I heard Pete screech "you rascal!" He must have picked that up from Will Will's mom when she was scolding him for getting into trouble.

Will Will's mom — Mrs. Peterson — gave him a hard time whenever he misbehaved, but she was a super lady in almost every way. First of all, she was good looking. Her face had a few wrinkles, but her eyes, nose and mouth were as pretty as a movie star's. She was tall and lean with whip-cord muscles and had enough pep and know-how to do almost anything.

Wearing ragged blue jeans and a faded flannel shirt, she'd mow or rake her whole yard without stopping. When her back porch got old and rickety, she built a new one that would have wowed the best carpenter in town.

Her sense of humor was also neat because she had a zany way of explaining things. I got one of those explanations one day when she was mowing her lawn. The mower ran out of gas and her gas can was empty, so I offered to ride my bike home to get some more. She thanked me and said it would be easier to siphon gas out of her car's tank by using a long hose.

She stuck one end of the hose into the tank, sucked a little on the other end, then held it in an upside-down "U." I was surprised to see the gas flowing into the empty can.

"How come the gas is running uphill through the hose?" I asked in amazement. "Because it has **sticktoativity**," she laughed. "Once it starts climbing, it always hangs on to itself so it won't fall back and get hurt." She was pulling my leg, of course, but I was only a kid then and didn't know whether to believe her or not.

Naturally, Will Will's mom was one of the reasons his place was so much fun. However, there were a few weird things about her. There was nothing unusual about the full-time work she did at Freeman's shoe factory because she was the only support her family had after her husband left her two years earlier. But the factory didn't pay enough, so she made ends meet by dressing pheasants, geese and ducks shot by hunters who wanted to cook and eat them.

If you went over to her house on a Friday or Saturday night in October or November, you'd probably find her in the basement scalding, de-feathering and de-gutting dozens of those birds. When she was finished, she'd dump all the leftover mess into a big patch of weeds behind her garage. If you asked her why, she'd laugh and say that all the stray cats in the neighborhood needed food. She'd also insist that they thanked her for being so generous.

The hunters paid her for cleaning their birds, of course. However, they also let her keep and cook a few. Once in a while they'd even bring her a raccoon or a ground hog or a possum. Since she was always looking for ways to stretch her grocery money, she'd cook these animals, too. I thought that was kind of gross – especially when Will Will invited me over for dinner one Sunday.

"What're we gonna have?" I asked as we pedaled our bikes along the gravel road that ran between my house and his.

"Possum," Will Will replied. "Old Man Wickler brought us a big fat one he bagged yesterday when he was out shooting pheasants. Mom's cooking it up right now with onions and potatoes and carrots. We'll have a real feast!"

Will Will was used to his mom's weird meals, so he took it for granted that I'd be tickled, too. I wasn't, because I'd read a wildlife book that made me think possums were vultures with fur instead of feathers. They'd eat all kinds of dead stuff, the book said, and they didn't care whether the stuff had been laying around for two minutes or two weeks.

As we rode toward Will Will's place, I tried to think of a good reason for pedaling back home. I would have told him my family was leaving for a vacation in an hour. However, he'd been at my house most of the day and hadn't seen anyone packing. Pretending to have terrible leg cramps wouldn't work, either, because we were heading down a hill that led to Will Will's driveway. We could coast right up to his front door.

I'd just have to sit down at the table and hope my stomach stayed where it was supposed to.

When I saw the cooked possum, I was sure I was going to heave. It was brownish yellow and looked like a big skinned cat as it lay on a platter piled high with potatoes, carrots and onions. It had a strong greasy odor that almost knocked me out of my chair.

"Dig in, everybody!" Will Will's mom sang out as she passed me the platter.

I forked a little piece of possum and covered it with two potatoes so she wouldn't notice I hadn't taken much. Then I handed the platter to Will Will. He helped himself to a hunk of meat and three or four potatoes and onions. Dan and Polly took their share, too. Soon all you could hear were teeth chomping food, and knives and forks scraping plates.

Everyone was so busy gulping and grabbing second helpings that I had no trouble dropping my piece of possum onto the floor. I knew nobody would ever find it because a couple of cats were cruising around under the table.

"Well, Johnny, how did you like your dinner?" asked Will Will's mom after the possum and all of the vegetables had disappeared.

"It was great, Mrs. Peterson!" I lied, patting my stomach. "Whew! I'm really stuffed."

She laughed and said she was glad I was able to come over. I felt pretty bad about fooling her, but I thought it was better to fib than to get sick and spoil everyone's dinner.

After the possum feast, Will Will and I went outside, looking for something to do. We walked from the backyard to the driveway in the front yard and saw Dan fiddling with his broken-down jalopy. I didn't want to be around him because he always acted like he was better than everyone else. Will Will thought Dan was annoying, too, but he decided to stop and see what big brother was doing.

Let me tell you some stuff about Dan so you'll be ready for the guff he gave us as we watched him pretending to be an auto mechanic.

A junior in high school, he was almost six feet tall and had a stocky build. His muscles weren't very large, but he'd flex them whenever he thought someone was admiring his body. His face was narrow, his chin was square, and his nose was hooked like a hawk's beak. He was sure he was super-handsome. In case some dimwit needed more proof, Dan would get a fancy buzz-cut whenever he went to the barber.

Dan also made fun of people by telling them lies about terrible trouble they were about to have.

Will Will and I fell into this trap as we watched Dan pounding dents out of one of the doors of his junker. Without expecting an ambush, we asked him if we'd enjoy ourselves when we got to high school.

"Hell, no!" he smirked, as flakes of paint flew off the door he was whacking. "You guys will sure wish you'd stayed in grade school as soon as you become freshmen."

I should have ignored that nonsense, but uneasiness mixed with curiosity got the best of me. "Why won't we like being freshmen?" I blurted.

"Because you'll have to put up with awful kinds of initiation," Dan replied, grinning like he'd just hit a jackpot. "Juniors and seniors take freshmen out to cemeteries on the darkest nights and make them jump over tombstones. That really scares them."

"That can't be very scary," said Will Will, as he stood on a hub cap Dan had tossed on the grass.

"Oh yes it can," Dan insisted. "The juniors and seniors jump up from behind the tombstones and howl like ghosts! Some of the freshmen crap their pants, they're so terrified."

"Yikes!" I exclaimed. "That's really gross!"

"It's even worse for freshman boys after gym class," laughed Dan. "The juniors and seniors wait 'til they come out of the shower, then shove them bare naked out the locker room door into the hall. About a hundred girls see them and laugh!"

Will Will and I were only in sixth grade, so we wouldn't have to worry about that kind of stuff for another three years. But Dan could tell I was upset.

"Then of course there's all the homework," he said, grabbing a rusty wrench tangled in the grass. "High school kids have to read and write a ton of stuff every night. If they don't have their work ready the next day, they get sent down to the principal!"

"Wha—What's the principal do?" I asked nervously.

Dan held the wrench up close to my face and pretended to twist my nose with it. "He punishes kids in lots of horrible ways! You'll find out real quick when you get to high school!"

Will Will stomped on a rusty can laying in the driveway. Then he kicked it half way to the road and said, "I don't believe that stuff about homework, Dan! If high school kids have so much of it, how come you never bring any home?"

Dan dropped his wrench and fumbled around for a few seconds before he picked it up again. "The teachers ease up on you when you get to be a junior," he replied. "And I do all my homework in study hall."

"But Mom said your teachers say you don't even —."

Will Will was turning the tables on Dan, and truth was about to clobber him. "You guys get out of here!" he snarled. "I gotta finish pounding this door, and I can't do it with a couple of twerps yacking at me."

We decided we'd better find something else to do, so we cut a couple of willow switches and started whipping the tops off thistles behind the garage. "You didn't swallow any of those lies — did you Johnny?" asked Will Will as he laid into a really big thistle.

I had swallowed most of them, but I was too embarrassed to say so. "Heck no!" I fibbed. "Only a moron would believe that junk about jumping over tombstones and getting shoved naked into the hall. But I sure hope that terrible principal never gets his hands on me!"

You're probably thinking that the title of this story — "Will Will's Fun Place" — isn't really true because Dan did bad things. Well, his mom's neat words and actions more than made up for his annoying behavior.

His and Will Will's little sister Polly is another reason you'd enjoy visiting Will Will's place. She was six years old and had a cute rounded nose. Her lips were just long and thick enough to fit perfectly between smooth, rounded cheeks. Her blue eyes were pretty, too, but in an unusual way. They angled up sharply on each side of her nose, then curved quickly downward toward the ends of her eyebrows. Long brown hair hung over her shoulders and framed her face.

Polly often looked happy — especially when she sang nonsense songs like the Will Will ditty. That was the one that lodged in my brain in fourth grade and made me shout the special name that stuck to her fun-famous brother.

Polly also had a habit of wrinkling her forehead, narrowing her eye lids, and pursing her lips when she looked at people. She was sizing them up. If you asked her what she was seeing or thinking, she'd tell you right away. She never mangled the truth like her brother Dan did. Her words might sound like compliments or insults, but they were always honest.

That's what happened one day when Will Will and I and three other guys were digging an underground fort behind his garage. Polly was watching, dressed in baggy jeans and a tattered sweater with cute little ponies on the front. Her eyes followed the swing of our shovels as we tossed dirt out of the hole.

Then she stared at Davy Schuster. That puzzled Will Will, so he asked her if Davy was doing something he shouldn't. "No," Polly answered. "He just has his pants unzipped. I can see inside them."

Davy blushed, and the rest of us laughed. Nothing else would have happened, however, if he'd just closed his fly and kept on digging. Instead, he dropped his shovel and yelled, "Don't make fun of me, you creeps. I just forgot to close my barn door!"

Will Will felt insulted and decided to needle Davy. "Hey, Polly," he yelled. "What else do you see that's bad about him?"

All of us expected to hear "nothing," but Polly frowned and said, "He's not wearing underpants."

Davy was a dead duck. He swore he had them on like everyone else, but he was blushing so bad that we knew Polly was right. "If your skivvies are in there, pull down your britches and prove it!" Ben Fredericks demanded.

"Yeah! Or we'll pull them down for you," Zack Kramer threatened.

"No you won't!" yelled Davy. "I'm going home."

He took off running toward the front yard where he'd left his bike, but we tackled him before he was even half way there. Four of us held down his arms and legs so he couldn't punch or kick, and Will Will yanked his trousers down below his knees.

"Hey, Davy!" he shouted, pretending to be really surprised. "You're not wearing underpants. Somebody must have swiped them when you weren't looking."

When we let Davy up, he was so mad he started swinging with both fists. He would have pounded all of us if he could have reached us. His trousers were still down, so we had no trouble keeping away from him. I could describe exactly what he looked like, but I'm sure your imagination's good enough to fill in the details.

In about a minute Davy calmed down enough to pull up his pants. He was cussing a blue streak as he jumped on his bike. As he rode out of the yard, he gave us the finger and yelled he'd get even with us.

"What do you suppose he'll do?" I asked Will Will.

"Nothing. He'll forget what we did to him and come back tomorrow and help us finish the fort."

We didn't see Davy again, but we were sure he'd been back because our fort got wrecked two days later. Then a day after that, we discovered someone had tied about a dozen knots in a rope ladder we used to climb up into the club house in the big willow tree in Will Will's back yard.

"It's gotta be Davy!" growled Will Will. "He must be coming around at night. We've got to catch that sneaky rat!"

We decided to camp out and wait for Davy. We'd set up an old tent by the tree and hide in it while we watched the back yard. Davy would show up right after dark, we figured, so we'd jump out and beat him to a pulp. Then we'd have the rest of the night to listen to hoot owls and tell each other ghost stories.

Everything would've worked out fine if we'd been able to stay awake. However, we'd worn ourselves out that day by tramping along some railroad tracks that ran way out into the country. As soon as we climbed into the tent at sunset, we fell asleep. The next thing we knew, it was morning.

"Hey!" yelled Will Will as he kicked off his blanket. "How come the tent's all sagged down?"

"Huh?" I mumbled, still half asleep.

Will Will sat up, pushed the top of the tent away from his head, and yelled, "Someone must've cut all the ropes on the sides. The only thing holding this sucker up are the two end poles!"

We crawled out and found that the ropes were OK, but all the stakes they were tied to had been pulled out of the ground.

I thought it was kind of funny, but Will Will was hopping mad. "That creep Davy yanked the stakes, and he's gonna die!" he snarled, smacking his fist into the palm of his other hand. "We'll get him tonight for sure!"

I thought we'd wait in the tent again, but Will Will said he had a better idea. "We'll set the tent back up, then climb up into the club house. Then when Davy comes back after dark, we'll swing down and knock him galley-west."

"I'm not sure we can pull that off," I said. "Davy may not go near the tent tonight."

"Oh, yes he will 'cause we'll leave out some cookies beside it for bait. Mom just baked a scrumptious batch, and we can sneak some out of the kitchen when she's not looking."

"But what will we swing down on?"

"I've got two long ropes in the basement. We'll tie them up in the tree right after breakfast."

The ropes looked like they'd work OK, but we had an awful time tying them up. We had to climb high into the tree to find just the right branches. About a million little twigs were waiting to scratch us to pieces. Then I almost fell when Will Will accidentally stomped on my fingers. But we did get the job done.

Next, we tested the ropes. We wanted to swing down together and really bash Davy as he picked up the cookies, so we figured we'd have to start from the top level of the club house.

We grabbed the ropes, and on the count of three we leaped out of the tree. We swung down so fast we couldn't see where we were headed — until we crashed down in the middle of the tent. Luckily it was made of strong canvas and didn't tear, but both end poles snapped in two.

"We'll try jumping from the lowest part of the club house," said Will Will as we cut new poles from a scrubby cottonwood beside the garage. "That way we'll know if we can whap Davy instead of the tent."

The ropes worked fine from the first level, so we knew we were ready to really clobber Davy. After supper we climbed back up in the tree to wait for him. Just as it was getting dark, we saw him sneak into the yard. He stopped right beneath us and looked around for about five seconds. Then he spotted the cookies and ran over to the tent.

"He's gonna take the bait!" whispered Will Will.

We'd been lying flat on our stomachs, looking over the edge of the clubhouse floor. As we stood up and reached for the ropes, I was afraid we'd make noise and spook Davy, but he didn't hear anything. He was just reaching for the cookies when we swung down at him.

If we had clobbered Davy, we probably would've put him in the hospital, so I guess it was a good thing we hit each other instead. Somehow our ropes got twisted, and we slammed together about a foot off the ground. I must have been knocked cold for a couple of seconds because the next thing I knew I was flat on my back, looking up at the stars.

I had no idea what had happened to Will Will and Davy until I sat up and saw them fighting beside the tent. They were rolling around, punching and kicking and yelling like a couple of wild animals. I would have jumped in and helped Will Will, but I didn't want to catch a fist or a foot in the face.

Suddenly I heard Will Will's mom shouting from the back porch. "Hey you two galoots! Knock it off!"

The next instant she was standing over Will Will and Davy. Before you could say "John Jacob Jingle," she grabbed both of them by their shirts and pulled them to their feet.

They kept right on fighting, so she shook them really hard.

"I said knock it off! Just what are you nitwits fighting about?"

The two fighters were all out of breath, so I had to do the talking. I told her that we had pulled down Davy's trousers a few days ago and that Davy had wrecked our fort, tied knots in our rope ladder, and yanked up our tent stakes to get even. I also said that Polly had started the whole thing by telling everyone Davy's fly was open.

Mrs. Peterson had looked really mad before I started explaining, so naturally I thought she was going to tan somebody's britches. But when she heard the part about Polly, she just laughed.

"You guys are knocking each other side ways and crooked over nothing! You're acting like a couple of yahoos. Let's all go inside and cool off and see if we can straighten everything out."

When we got in the house, Will Will's mom made popcorn. Will Will and Davy just glared at each other as they ate it, but pretty soon they shook hands and said they'd be friends again. Then Mrs. Peterson drove Davy home. Will Will and I went outside and climbed into the tent to get some sleep.

Before I nodded off, I thought about all the stuff we'd done that day. We'd made special rope swings and wrecked and repaired a tent. Then we'd caught a person who'd been playing nasty tricks on us. Finally, we'd learned that it's stupid to fight about something a little kid says.

"A great day at Will Will's place," I told myself as I fell asleep.

SIX:
Will Will Helps Out — Really!

Most grownups who knew Will Will thought he was a wild kid who wouldn't amount to much. "What good is he?" they'd ask each other. "All he does is act crazy and cause trouble." Well, there were a few times when Will Will did nice things for other people. Like the time he spent one whole day helping me with chores.

It was a Saturday in April when we were in eighth grade. Mom was starting her spring house cleaning, and I got dragged into it. She said I had to beat throwrugs, move furniture, and take down storm windows.

Dad was supposed to do these jobs, but he'd gotten wind of Mom's cleaning plans on Friday and decided to go fishing. My brother Sam was too young to do heavy work, so Mom was really depending on me.

As I walked out into the front yard after breakfast, I realized I'd be slaving all day in beautiful spring weather. A few puffy clouds hung in the sky, but the sun was bright, and a hawk was spinning big, slow circles high overhead. A light wind rustled the leaves of the tall cottonwood at the end of our driveway. That was a pleasant sound, but so was the "wheet! wheet! wheet!" of a bright red cardinal at the top of the walnut tree near our front door.

"Cryminee!" I said to myself as I trudged back into the house to start my boring chores. I had to force myself to drag ten rugs out into the backyard to beat the dust out of them.

Just as I threw the last rug over a clothes line, I heard a familiar rattling. Looking around, I saw Will Will pumping up the driveway on his beat-up old bike. Its fenders and chain guard were loose, and a couple of spokes in its back wheel were bent. He never fixed that bike, but somehow it held together.

Will Will was steering with one hand and holding his basketball against his side with the other. As he rode across the lawn, he flipped the ball to me.

"C'mon, Johnny! Let's ride to town and shoot some baskets at the school playground!" he shouted.

"I can't. Mom's got a whole slug of work for me," I moaned. "I have to start by pounding these stupid rugs!"

"The heck with that! Tell your mom you're gonna play basketball now and wallop rugs later."

"She'll say I can't go."

"Well, ask her anyway, you moron! She just might say 'yes'."

I said I'd give it a try and trudged through the back porch into the kitchen while Will Will waited outside, near the door.

Mom was standing on a step ladder, holding a bucket of sudsy water and scrubbing grease from the wall behind the stove. I could tell she wasn't in a very good mood because she frowned when she saw me.

"I hope you're not going to tell me you've finished the rugs already!" she said in a cranky way. "The broom's still here in the corner, so I know you haven't beaten them yet."

"No, but I've hung all the rugs on the clothes lines," I answered, trying to soften her up for the big question. "Can I go up to the school and shoot baskets with Will Will for a little while, Mom? He's outside with his bike and ball waiting for me."

Mom threw her rag into the scrub pail and climbed down from the ladder. Then she shook her finger within an inch of my face. It looked like a billy club that was about to scramble my brains.

"I'm sick and tired of hearing about Will Will, Johnny!" she griped. "Every time I ask you to do some work around here, you want to run off with that trouble maker."

"Shhh, Mom," I whispered. "He's standing on the back porch where he can hear you."

"I don't care! All he does is get you into scrapes. You haven't forgotten about that awful 'Yankees and Confederates' game, have you? And what about that monkey business with the slingshots and that shellacking you got from farmer Beatty? You'd be a lot better off if you stayed away from that **scamp!**"

I wasn't surprised when Mom mentioned the rotten-apple game and the slingshots, since the school and Old Man Benson had called her about them. But I just about pooped my pants when she brought up the whipping Old Man Beatty had given us. Will Will and I had done our best to keep it a secret, but someone must've spilled the beans.

Anyway, Mom's dander was up. I knew it wouldn't do any good to say anything else, so I grabbed the broom and went back outside.

Will Will was sitting on the top step of the porch with his head down on his arms, which were resting on his knees. He looked sick.

"You OK?" I asked. He didn't move for about five seconds. When he looked up, I could see his eyes were kind of red.

"I'm just a little tired 'cause I got to bed late last night," he answered in sort of a sad voice. Then he laughed and said, "Say, Johnny, why don't I give you a hand with your chores? We can shoot baskets any old time."

I couldn't believe what I was hearing! Will Will had never liked to do anything that wasn't fun, but now he was offering to get mixed up in a whole bunch of boring jobs.

"C'mon! You're pulling my leg!" I said. "I've got about a hundred crummy things to do, and you're standing around trying to be a comedian."

"No kidding! I want to help you out," Will Will insisted. "Got another broom?"

I would have asked why he wanted to work his butt off, but I didn't want to push my luck. If he was crazy enough to give up basketball for rugs and furniture and storm windows, I wasn't going to gripe!

We got another broom from the garage, and soon both of us were whacking the rugs like mad men. Dust flew out in big gray clouds and made us sneeze, but we enjoyed hearing the "whuup, whuup, whuup" of the brooms as they punished the rugs for being so full of grit.

"What in the world's going on out here!" called Mom from the back porch. She was standing with her hands on her hips, looking like she'd just seen a ghost.

"Hi, Mrs. Hyland!" shouted Will Will, waving his broom over his head. "We'll have these rugs clean as a whistle in a jiffy. Then we'll get busy at something else."

It took Mom at least ten seconds to get over the shock of seeing Will Will working. When she was able to speak, she motioned for me to come over to the porch.

"What's wrong with Will Will?"

"Nothing that I know of. He's just helping me with my chores."

"Since when has that scamp done anything useful? He must be planning to play some kind of crazy trick on us! You'd better tell him to go home."

"Aw, Mom," I pleaded. "Let him stay. I don't think he'll try anything funny. But I'll keep an eye on him just in case. OK?"

"Well, you're responsible for whatever trouble he causes. I don't trust him!"

I watched Will Will closely, but he didn't fool around at all. Instead, he pounded the rugs so fast I could hardly keep up with him. As soon as we'd beaten the last one, he dashed into the kitchen to ask Mom what we could do next. I leaned the brooms against the garage, then ran after him. As soon as I got to the porch, Mom came out and started whispering to me.

"Maybe I was a bit hard on Will Will, Johnny," she said, looking sheepish. "He's acting so polite, and he just said you two would move all the furniture in the house so I can do all the cleaning without stopping. I'm still a little suspicious, but it looks like he really wants to help. You'd better get busy before he changes his mind."

Mom told us we could start by carrying all of the stuff from the living room out onto the front lawn. Before you could say "Jacky Robinson," Will Will was lifting one end of Dad's big easy chair.

"Shake a leg, Johnny!" he grunted. "I can't hoist this monster all by myself." I grabbed the other end, and in about twenty seconds the chair was setting on the grass beside the front door.

Just as we'd set the chair down, a guy named Dan Edwards who lived down the road drove past in his old rattle-trap truck.

I turned and waved at him. When I looked back toward the house, Will Will had vanished. Naturally I thought he'd run away. "I should have known he wouldn't last," I muttered as I walked back toward the front door.

"Move it or lose it!" shouted a voice from inside the door. I jumped to one side just in time to keep from getting knocked flat by the top end of Mom's wooden rocking chair. Will Will was carrying it upside down on his shoulders, with his head poking up through the space between its seat and the four strips of wood that formed its back rest.

"You're falling behind, old buddy!" he said in a smart-alecky way.

I was happy to see he hadn't left, but I didn't like the way he zinged me. "Is that so?" I answered, just as smart alecky. "I can work circles around you any day, Mr. Superman!"

For the next fifteen minutes we worked our butts off, seeing who could tote the most furniture. I hauled out two end tables, a magazine rack, a flower vase and an empty bookcase. Will Will lugged a foot stool, a plant stand, a floor lamp and a coat rack.

We had to work together getting the couch and the TV cabinet out the door. Then we tried to outdo each other again by hauling everything back into the living room after Mom had finished cleaning it. About twenty minutes later we had most of the kitchen stuff out on the back porch, when Mom made us ease up.

"You boys must be wearing yourselves to a frazzle!" she called. "Sit down and have some milk and cookies."

I could tell that Mom was grateful for the help Will Will was giving us, but she wasn't sure he'd stay until all the work was done. Her doubt almost vanished, however, when she saw how he hustled when we moved the furniture out of the bedrooms. I could tell that he had almost won her over because she invited him to stay for lunch and fed him hot dogs and potato chips and ice cream for dessert.

By about three in the afternoon Mom had cleaned all the rooms in the house, and by about four o'clock we had everything carried back into them. Now only the outside storm windows were left.

I shouldn't say "only" because there were ten windows, and everyone was big and clunky. Our house was just one story, so we thought we could get all of them down by using a step ladder. But there were lots of flower beds in the way. Rows of daffodils had glaring yellow blossoms that seemed to threaten us if we got too close. The tulips behind those angry daffs had so many red and pink petal cups that we wondered how we'd get past them.

We straddled the flowers carefully with the ladder and tried to finish our last chore without any trouble. Will Will stood on the ladder and undid the hooks at the bottom of each window. Then he swung the windows out and lifted them off the metal pieces that had held them in place at the top of the window frames.

I grabbed the windows as Will Will lowered them, then tip-toed out of the flower beds to lean them against the garage. We planned to wait until all the windows were down, then carry them to the basement.

Both of us were dog tired, but we figured we could finish before supper time. Then we blew it. It really wasn't our fault — just a foul-up that could happen to anyone.

Will Will had just pulled the ninth window off the house and was lowering it to me when it slipped out of his hands. I wasn't quick enough to grab it, so one corner hit the ground. It didn't seem to land very hard, but all of the glass flew out in little pieces like someone had bashed it with a hammer.

Just then I noticed Will Will having trouble. He was standing on the next-to-highest step on the ladder, swinging his arms around in big circles, trying to keep his balance. "Whoa! Whoa! Whoa!" he hollered as he swayed back and forth.

Unfortunately, we were close to Mom's prize lilac bush, which was covered with big clusters of purple flowers. Will Will fell sideways off the ladder and tried to land on his feet, but his body twisted, and he did a perfect swan dive into the bush. That was many years ago, but the branches still snap and crackle in my memory. My mind also has a clear picture of Will Will thrashing around inside the bush.

He was lucky to have only a few scratches; but as soon as he climbed out, he started crying. At first he just sniffled a little. In about ten seconds he was sitting on the grass, bawling his head off.

"Jeez, Will Will, what's the matter?" I asked, wondering what I could do. He laid his head down on his knees and kept bawling. Just then Mom came tearing around the house with an ornery look on her face.

"What's going on here?" she demanded. "I thought I heard glass breaking

and someone yelling!"

Before I could say anything, she spotted the busted window and mangled lilac. "Oh, no! Look at this mess! How'd you rascals manage to do all this damage?"

She was ready to give us a good tongue lashing when Will Will spoke up. "It's all my fault, Mrs. Hyland, and I'm awful sorry!" he sobbed. "I've been trying all day to help out so you'd stop thinking I'm a scamp. Then I really screwed up while we were finishing our chores!"

I explained how the accident happened and how Will Will could have been hurt really bad when he fell off the ladder.

When Mom knew the real reason Will Will was crying, she felt terrible. "I'm really sorry I called you a trouble maker!" she said, kneeling down beside him. "You're a little wild, but you're really a good boy. I appreciate everything you've done to help us today, and I'm not angry about the window or the bush."

Will Will smiled and rubbed his eyes. "You're sure you're not mad at me?"

"Not a bit, and I want you to know you're always welcome to come over to our house. But I think you'd better go home now. It's getting late, and your mother must be wondering where you are."

"Yippee!" shouted Will Will as he jumped to his feet. He did a little high-step tap dance before hopping on his bike and pedaling down the driveway. Before he reached the road, Mom noticed he'd left his basketball.

"Will Will!" she called. "You forget your ball!"

"That's OK," he shouted back. "Johnny can give it to me tomorrow. We're gonna spend the whole day up at the playground shooting baskets!"

SEVEN:
Snagging Mr. Whiskers

After Mom found out that Will Will had a good side, she never complained when I wanted to do things with him. And sometimes she even thought up special ways for us to have fun. She came up with a really good idea about a week after the big spring-cleaning day while our family was eating supper.

We'd just finished passing the potatoes around when she looked at Dad and said, "John, why don't you take Johnny and Will Will fishing this weekend?"

Mom wanted Will Will and me to enjoy ourselves, but I suspect she was also trying to teach Dad a lesson. He had a habit of running off to the Rock River with his poles and tackle box when she had work for him around the house.

That was why Will Will and I became the fill-in house cleaners that you read about in the last story. If Dad had to take us fishing now, our live-wire antics would punish him for weaseling out of that big adventure with rugs, furniture and windows.

If that's what Mom was thinking, Dad must've been thinking it, too, because he almost choked on a mouthful of brussel sprouts. "Taking the boys to the river isn't a good idea," he sputtered.

"Yes it is!" I protested. "We'd have a great time."

Dad frowned, but Mom smiled. "Johnny and Will Will would learn a lot about fishing, John. Aren't you the one who says kids should be good at outdoor sports?"

Mom had Dad cornered, but he wasn't ready to give up. "The boys already know how to fish," he argued. "Remember all those bluegills they caught last month from Dan Edwards' pond?"

"Aw, Dad! Anyone can snag those little squirts. We want to be able to catch catfish, like those big hollocurs you call Mr. Whiskers. You'll take us to the river, won't you?"

Dad knew he was licked, so he sighed and said, "OK. We'll go this Saturday. But you and Will Will better not horse around!"

Dad was grumpy when he realized he had to go fishing with Will Will and me, but he was usually good natured. If you behaved yourself when you were with him, he'd be happy to do things to help you — like teaching you how to cut grass with a big power mower, or how to save money you'd earned peddling newspapers. He didn't laugh much when you were learning, but he enjoyed shaping you up.

Dad also liked to watch sports like baseball and football on TV. He wasn't the athletic type, however. He didn't swim, play tennis, jog, or even pitch horse shoes. His shift work at our town's huge steam plant wore him out. On his days off, he insisted on doing quiet and relaxing things — like fishing alone. That's why he was grouchy when he realized he'd have to enjoy his next river trip with two fidgety fellows tagging along.

I was so glad that Dad had agreed to take us that I called Will Will right after supper. He was happy, too, but he thought we had to do a lot of work to get ready for Saturday.

"We only have three days to get all our fishing stuff around!" Will Will declared. "We've got to check our gear, practice casting, and dig worms. This is our big chance to do some real fishing, and we want to be ready!"

Our gear was in bad shape. Both of us had old-fashioned open-faced reels, and the lines on them were snarled. We pulled out all the tangles. Then we discovered that the reels would hardly turn.

"We must have gotten a ton of sand in these suckers the last time we fished at Dan's pond," Will Will complained. "We'll have to take them all apart and clean them up." We spread the parts of the reels out on Will Will's basement floor. We wiped them off and oiled them and were starting to put them back together. Just then Rex, Will Will's big collie, came tearing down the steps. Before we could stop him, he was jumping all over us, wanting to play.

Will Will grabbed Rex by the collar and hauled him back upstairs. By then, all our reel parts were mixed up and scattered in six or seven directions. It took about an hour to find everything and figure out where it was supposed to go.

When we looked at our poles, we saw that the threads around the line guides had come loose. We re-wrapped them, then inspected our tackle boxes. You can imagine how we felt when we discovered a whole bunch of dried-up worms inside. They stuck like glue to the sides of the boxes and to all our hooks and bobbers.

"Holy Toledo!" growled Will Will. "How're we gonna get everything loose?"

"With our fingers, of course."

"No way! I'm not gonna touch that stinking mess. We'll just pour hot water into the boxes and soften everything up."

The hot water dissolved the worms, but little pieces of gunk were still on our hooks. Will Will thought we should clean them with sandpaper or steel wool.

"Why bother?" I asked. "Dad says catfish eat chicken guts and lots of rotten stuff. They won't mind if our hooks have some crud on them."

Will Will thought that made sense, so we started working on our casting. We knew we'd have to be able to heave our lines a long way because Dad said our fishing spot would be far out in the river. "We gotta tie something heavy to our lines so we can really get some distance," Will Will declared. "We won't need hooks while we practice, but we gotta have some weight. What can we use?"

We found two big padlocks in an old battered cabinet. They worked fine tied to our lines because we were able to cast them clear across Will Will's front yard. But we couldn't throw them exactly where we wanted. Will Will's line sailed high up into a tree when he tried to hit the trunk. My line was supposed to hit a telephone pole, but the padlock I was using banged the side of the house, just half an inch from a big window.

I was afraid we'd have trouble aiming our lines when we got to the river, but Will Will said we wouldn't have to drop them right in front of fish. "They'll swim around 'til they find our bait, so it's no big deal if we're not perfect casters."

Getting worms was no problem. We picked up about two dozen from under a big pile of leaves Will Will's Mom had left behind the garage when she'd raked the yard the year before. Two old empty coffee cans happened to be laying beside the leaf pile. We put the worms in them and were ready to go fishing.

Will Will and I were up bright and early Saturday morning. We had our poles, tackle boxes and worm cans packed in Dad's car by 6:30, but we had to wait another hour until he got out of bed. After Mom made us a big pancake and sausage breakfast, we were off to the river.

"We're really gonna have fun today," sang Will Will as we rode down a narrow dirt road that led to Dad's fishing spot. Dad wasn't excited. He just said "Hmmf!" as he steered the car toward the river.

It was hard to tell where we were because there was nothing but bushes and big trees all along the road. Branches kept brushing against the car. We couldn't see the river until we came around a curve and almost ran into it. The road stopped at the edge of the water, so all we had to do was climb out and start fishing. At least that's what Will Will and I thought as we grabbed our gear.

"Wait a second, you guys!" said Dad in a grouchy voice. "Catching catfish takes patience. You've got to sit still and wait until they bite."

"We've got all kinds of patience," bubbled Will Will, hopping up and down with excitement. "We just can't wait to get going!"

When Dad saw our poles, he smiled a little. "And you have to have the right kind of tackle. You won't catch much with huge padlocks tied on your lines above your hooks."

"They worked great when we were casting without the hooks in Will Will's yard, Dad. We figured we could use them in the river, too."

Dad told us to take off the padlocks and hooks. Then he opened his tackle box and gave each of us a lead sinker with a little wire loop at the top.

"Stick your lines through the loops," he told us. "Then pull out enough line so you can tie your hooks on again."

"This sinker's no good!" Will Will complained. "Its loop's so big it'll slide right down on top of my hook when I cast."

"No it won't," Dad explained, holding out a handful of lead B-B's with little notches in them. "These are split shots. Clamp one of them onto your line below the sinker, about a foot above your hook. The split shot's bigger that the loop, so it'll keep the sinker up where it's supposed to be."

Will Will's tongue was sticking out the side of his mouth, so I knew he was doing some serious thinking. The next instant he was talking a mile a minute.

"That's really neat, Mr. Hyland! The sinker can't go past the split shot, but the line will slip through the loop when a fish grabs the bait and pulls it out. What a great invention!"

I would've laughed and asked Will Will if the sinkers and split shots were as great as his rotten-apple trap invention, but I didn't want to remind Dad of the trouble we'd gotten into in fifth grade. He was starting to act like he was enjoying himself, so I thought I'd better let sleeping dogs lie.

Dad told us to put our worms on our hooks while he cut some forked sticks to prop up our poles on the river bank after our lines were in the water. Then he pointed to a huge bunch of dead branches sticking out of the river about forty yards from shore.

"We're going to drop our lines just below that big snag," he said. "Can you guys throw yours that far?"

"No problem, Dad. Didn't I tell you we've been practicing our casting?"

"OK, son. Give it a try."

I grabbed my pole with both hands and raised it high over my left shoulder. Then I took a deep breath and whipped it forward. I expected to see my line go flying straight toward the snag. It looped high in the air, then plopped into the water only about four feet from shore.

"Ahem!" said Dad. "My turn!" shouted Will Will.

Will Will's line went sailing all the way out to the snag, and his bait and sinker landed in the middle of it. When he gave the line a flip, it got tangled in the branches. Then when he tried to yank it loose, it broke.

I thought Dad would be upset at losing one of his special sinkers, but he just gave Will Will another one, along with another split shot. "Put on another hook, too, and bait up again," he said.

Dad didn't want us to mess up again, so he threw both of our lines out for us. "There!" he declared. "That ought to be just the right spot to snag Mr. Whiskers. Now prop your poles up and wait until he grabs your bait. And be patient! Any questions?"

"Yeah," said Will Will. "Do catfish have real whiskers? Are they made of hair, and are they real long and gray like the beards old guys have?"

"Whaat? Hee! Hee! Hoh! Hoh! Hah! Hah! Hah!"

I'd never seen Dad laugh so hard. Mom called him "Mr. Sobersides" because he laughed only about once a week. Here he was, gasping and wheezing like he'd just heard the world's funniest joke.

"I'm sorry," he finally said. "I just wasn't expecting that kind of question."

Will Will looked serious and said, "Well, do catfish have real whiskers?"

"No," Dad sputtered, trying to keep a straight face. "Their whiskers are really fleshy feelers that they use to find their way along the bottom of muddy rivers."

Dad threw his own line into the water, and all three of us sat down on the bank. Nobody said anything for about ten minutes. We just watched our lines and admired the river.

The water flowed past us in long ripples. It wasn't the only thing moving, however. About a dozen ducks with gray bodies and green heads paddled around the snag. They must have been fishing for something because they kept poking their bills down into the water. Some of the ducks even pushed their whole heads under, pointing their tails straight up into the air. In a few seconds their heads popped back out of the water, and they were paddling again.

Tiny brown birds were flitting around in the snag's dead branches. I couldn't get a good look at them because they were too far away. What I did see without any trouble were orange-bellied swallows zipping up and down above the river. Their wing tips almost touched the water as they swooped low to snatch gnats and flies. They were also zig zagging to keep from running into each other.

As I watched the zig-zagging bug snatchers, I almost forgot about my line. That wasn't a problem because nothing was taking the bait. Nothing was moving Will Will's line, either. Both of us got bored when we thought Mr. Whiskers was ignoring us.

Dad pulled the bill of his cap down over his eyes and laid back to take a nap. Will Will and I weren't sleepy, so we tossed a few pebbles into the river. Then we dumped our worms out on the bank to see if the ones we still had were still alive.

"Did you ever make a grass squawker?" asked Will Will as he fingered the worms.

"No. What is it?"

"Just a long blade of grass you hold between your thumbs and blow on. Here, I'll show you how."

Will Will held the grass in his slimy hands and blew a ear-piercing **SQUAWK!** It spooked a whole bunch of blackbirds in a bush behind us and scared the daylights out of Dad as the flock exploded into the sky.

"Hey, you guys!" he shouted, jumping to his feet. "You're not supposed to be horsing around!"

"But there's nothing biting, Dad. Maybe we should fish someplace else."

"I told you guys to be patient. Just sit still — and be **quiet!**"

Dad laid down again, and Will Will and I looked around for something else to do. All of a sudden we saw a frog hopping along the bank a few feet away. Both of us tried to grab it, but it escaped into a bunch of weeds.

"Hey, watch out!" yelled Will Will as I accidentally knocked him off balance. He started sliding down the bank on his butt, trying to dig in his heels to stay out of the water. He would have gotten soaked if I hadn't grabbed his arm. Only his shoes and pant cuffs got wet, but that was enough to tee him off.

"You clumsy jerk!" he shouted as I pulled him back up. "If I'd wanted to go swimming, I'd have brought my swimming suit!"

Dad heard the commotion, of course, and got upset again. "What's a person have to do to get a little rest?" he growled. "I knew it was a bad idea to bring you numb skulls fishing!"

He probably would have taken us right home, but just then Will Will's reel started clicking. Its handle was turning, which meant that something was pulling out his line.

"You've got a fish," Dad said quietly.

Will Will grabbed his pole and was about to give the line a yank, but Dad told him to let the fish go for several seconds to make sure it had swallowed the bait. Then he said "Pull!" and Will Will set the hook.

Whatever Will Will had snagged took off like a run-away submarine. It was all he could do to hang on to his pole. "Let out your line, or you'll lose the fish!" Dad called. He kept coaching, and Will Will followed his directions perfectly. He released his line every time the fish swam away, then cranked it back in whenever it slowed down. What he was battling must have been a real lunker because the water seemed to boil whenever it swam near the surface.

The fish fought for about five minutes before Will Will was able to pull it in close to the shore. Dad slid down the bank to the edge of the water and leaned out, ready to grab the monster. It splashed water all over him as he hooked his fingers under its gills. The next instant he was scrambling back up the bank on his hands and knees, dragging a huge cat with fins and a tail.

"Hurrah!" yelled Will Will as Dad held up his prize.

"Way to go, old buddy!" I shouted, slapping him on the back. "You just snagged Mr. Whiskers!"

The fish was about four feet long. By the way Dad was straining, it must have been pretty heavy. It had a big flat head and a thick, clunky body covered with shiny gray skin. It looked like some weird prehistoric creature.

Dad pulled a rope out of his tackle box and looped one end of it through the fish's gills and mouth. Then he knotted the other end around a tree and dropped the lunker back into the river to keep it alive until we went home. He'd just thrown Will Will's line back out near the snag when I yelled that I had a fish.

Mine was a catfish, too. It was smaller than Will Will's, so Dad didn't have as much trouble grabbing my prize. He barely had time to catch his breath, however, before Will Will snagged another Mr. Whiskers.

In about half an hour Will Will and I had caught three more fish and worn Dad to a frazzle. He was really sagging when we got into the car and headed home. As we bounced and bumped up the dirt road, we thanked him and said we had lots of fun.

"I could tell that," Dad mumbled, sounding completely bushed. "You guys are a couple of absolute live wires!"

Then Will Will asked a question that Dad must have known was coming. "Will you please take us fishing again next Saturday, Mr. Hyland?"

"I won't be able to," Dad replied. "Mrs. Hyland will want me to work around the house that day, and I'd sure hate to disappoint her."

EIGHT:
A Perfect Job?

About a year after Will Will and I learned to snag Mr. Whiskers, we decided to make some money. We didn't need it for any particular reason. However, there were always things like pellet guns and model airplanes and mail-order taxidermy courses we might want to buy.

We weren't sure how we'd earn our cash. Some kids delivered newspapers or sacked groceries, or even detasseled corn. We wanted a job that would be really interesting — and as easy as possible. The one we chose was pretty unusual.

It all started one hot summer morning when I was out in my backyard trying to find a slow leak in one of my bike tires. I'd pulled out the inner tube and was holding it down in a pail of water, looking for air bubbles coming from the leak. Suddenly someone snuck up behind me and clapped his hands over my eyes.

"Guess who?" said a gruff voice.

"C'mon, Will Will! I know it's you," I laughed.

"No it isn't! I'm a spaceman from the planet of Konframatory, and I'm gonna zoom off with you in my flying saucer!"

Before the "spaceman" could kidnap me, I threw a double handful of water over my shoulder. It must have hit him square in the face because he started coughing and sputtering.

I whirled around and pretended to be surprised. "Will Will! It is you. You really fooled me!"

Will Will was rubbing his eyes and trying to catch his breath, but he managed to mumble something about wise acres who deserved to be nabbed by real spacemen.

"Aw, don't be a sorehead!" I said. "You've got to admit you set yourself up for that water blast."

"Well, maybe I did, but you didn't have to drown me," growled Will Will. "OK, I'm sorry." I replied. "So what're you up to today?"

Will Will was still a little peeved when he said, "I came over to tell you I've just found a perfect job for us. But you're gonna have to guess what it is!"

I didn't like quiz games, but I decided to play along to cheer him up. I tried to think of something really ridiculous, so I asked, "Are we gonna be squirrel trainers or test pilots for pigeons?"

"You're not even close!" laughed Will Will. "Try harder."

"I'll bet we'll be selling snow shovels to people in the Sahara desert."

"Not in a million years!"

Now I was the one getting testy. "Aw, for crying out loud! Tell me what the stupid job is!"

"It's not stupid!" Will Will insisted. "We're gonna raise and sell rabbits!"

"That's about as loony as catching clouds or raising cockroaches," I replied. "How'd you think of something like that?"

Will Will said he'd gotten the idea the day before from Mike Reynolds, who wanted to sell him a rabbit-raising business. Mike said he'd been making lots of money selling rabbits to people who cooked and ate them. His family was moving to California, however, and it would be too much trouble to take all of the rabbits and their cages along.

I thought I smelled a rat, so I asked, "How'd Mike get a hold of you, and why did he want you to buy his business?"

"If you must know, he called me on the phone," said Will Will, looking disgusted. "He wanted to do me a favor because he knew I liked animals. I'm surprised you couldn't figure that out for yourself!"

"What I can't figure out is why Mike told you that stuff. He was hopping mad when we sprang the rotten-apple trap on him and his Yankees back in fifth grade. I'll bet he's held a grudge against us ever since."

Will Will rolled his eyes in disbelief. "How can you be such a Gloomy Gus, Johnny? Mike's not mad at us for clobbering him and his gang. I know he's not because he laughed when I asked him if he remembered all the fun we had in fifth grade. And he was really happy when I told him you might be part of the business."

"You might be right," I admitted. "But you'd better find out how much it's going to cost us — and whether the rabbit gig is really going to be perfect."

Will Will gave me a smug look and said, "You're worrying about nothing!

Mike said he'd let us have the whole kit and caboodle for only thirty dollars. He also said we could come over and look at his great setup this afternoon."

Mike lived about two miles out in the country on the other side of town, so we had a long, hot bike ride. When we got to his house, he was sitting on the front porch. As soon as he saw us pedaling up the driveway, he jumped up, waved, and shouted, "Hi, guys!"

I glanced at Mike, then did a double take. He didn't seem to be the same guy I knew four years ago when all of us got into the Yankees and Confederates mess. He'd changed schools after fifth grade, so I only had memories of him as the Yankee general.

I remembered how he scowled and shouted to egg his Yankees on as they chased us to the rotten apple trap during our last playground battle. I also had a brain picture of Mike yelling and pawing at his head to get the stinky apple goo out of his hair. The rest of the Yankees were in the picture, too, stumbling around after being blasted by Will Will's paper-bag cannon.

Now Mike looked like the most good-natured guy in the world. He had a wide, open-mouth grin that pushed his cheeks up and narrowed his eyes. His eyes sparkled, however, and his eyebrows arched high above them. He seemed like our best friend.

Mike's words of welcome were just as amazing. "I'm **really** happy to see you guys, and I'm sure you're gonna **love** what I've got for you," he gushed. "You won't be sorry if you buy my rabbits. They're real easy to take care of, and you'll be able to sell all the ones you raise to lots of people who'll enjoy cooking and eating them!"

After we leaned our bikes against the side of the porch, Mike told us to sit down on the steps. Then he hurried behind his house and came back carrying a huge white rabbit.

"This is Henrietta," he said as he set her on the lawn in front of us.

I expected to see Henrietta take off for parts unknown, but she just sat there, nibbling grass and twitching her nose.

"She's really tame," Mike assured us. "Go ahead and pet her."

He could see we liked Henrietta, so he let us stroke her back for about five minutes. Then he picked her up and told us to follow him. He led us through his backyard and behind his garage. We saw a long row of wire pens that stood on wooden legs about four feet off the ground.

Mike put Henrietta into the first pen, which was empty. Then he showed us two gray female rabbits named Annabel and Betty and one dark brown male called Ralph. All of them were in separate cages.

"I'm sure you guys have learned about the birds and the bees, so I don't need to explain how rabbits multiply," laughed Mike.

Will Will laughed, too. "We've learned enough to know that Ralph has to get together with Henrietta and Annabel and Betty to keep your business going."

"I put him in with them about once every three months," Mike explained. "About two months after that I get lots of babies — like these guys."

Mike was pointing to a big pen at the end of the row. Eleven gray, white and brown bunnies were hopping back and forth in it, with their ears pointing straight up. Every few seconds some of them would stop, sit back on their tails, and look around like they were waiting for something to happen. "It's a good thing they don't know they'll wind up in people's stomachs," I told myself.

Mike explained that the eleven hoppers were over half grown and would be ready to sell in about a month. "By that time you guys will be running the business, so all the money they bring in will be yours!" he promised.

Mike was trying his best to convince us that rabbit raising was a great job. However, he was careful not to make it sound too good to be true.

"Of course, you'll have to spend a little money once in a while," he explained. "For instance, you'll have to buy special food pellets for the rabbits to make sure they get enough vitamins and minerals."

"I didn't know that," I said. I might just as well have admitted that I knew nothing at all about rabbits, but I didn't want to sound like a moron.

"Don't worry," Mike replied. "You'll only have to give them a few pellets every day. Most of the time they'll eat grass. You can just set them out in your yard and they'll feed themselves for free so you won't have to spend a penny. And they'll cut your lawn, too!"

Mike said that everything we needed to know about rabbit raising was in a book called *Rabbit Production for Beginners.* We could have it without paying anything extra. He also promised to give us a list of all the people who'd bought rabbits from him. "You guys will never have to look for customers because everyone on the list will be begging for you to sell what you raise."

Mike was trying to sound really generous, so he said, "Since I really like you guys, Dad and I will load all the rabbits and their pens into his truck and bring them to wherever you plan to keep them."

Will Will and I had a little trouble deciding where that would be. His backyard was bigger than mine, so I figured the rabbits would be better off living there.

"Well, they wouldn't live long," warned Will Will. "As soon as we put them out on the lawn, all the cats would be after them. Old Max would just love to make Henrietta his next meal!"

We couldn't let that happen, of course, so I decided to tell Mike to bring everything to my house. But first I had to get my parents to agree.

"You and Will Will want to raise **what** in our backyard?" Mom asked when I told her about our new job. She'd just finished watching her favorite TV soap opera, so she was in a pretty good mood, but I could tell she wasn't too crazy about the idea.

"We want to get rabbits from an old pal named Mike Reynolds, and we want to keep them in pens along the back fence near your big flower bed," I explained. " They won't bother anything, and Will Will and I plan to raise and sell them and make lots of money."

"How many rabbits will you have?"

"Oh, just a few," I replied, stretching the truth a little."

"And how much will you earn?"

I figured that since I'd already told a tiny fib, one more wouldn't hurt. "We don't know what we'll get exactly, but it should be quite a bit. Mike said about a hundred people in town will be glad to buy and eat the rabbits when they're big enough to sell."

Mom thought we could be headed for trouble, but she said the rabbits could live in our yard if Dad said it was OK. All he said was "uhhh" because he was half asleep in his easy chair. I figured that meant "yes".

Now that we had a place for the rabbits, Will Will and I had to come up with the thirty dollars to pay for them. My young brother Sam had almost that much in his piggy bank, and we thought about borrowing it without telling him. However, we decided to earn the cash by mowing lawns for a bunch of old ladies that Will Will's grandma knew.

We made forty dollars in two weeks, so we had enough to pay Mike and buy rabbit pellets, too.

Mike and his dad delivered the rabbits and their cages the day before they left for California. They had to make three trips and lug everything from their truck into my back yard, but Mike didn't ask us to help. "Just relax and enjoy watching what we're doing," he said. "We want to make sure every thing's where it's supposed to be so you guys can jump right into your wonderful new business!"

Mike gave us the rabbit-raising book, but not the list of the people who would buy our rabbits. "I'd let you have it right now," he explained, "but I have to double check to make sure all the names are on it. I'll mail it to you in just a few days, as soon as I'm sure I didn't leave anybody out."

After shaking our hands, Mike wished us good luck. "I know you guys will have lots of fun," he laughed as he was leaving.

Will Will and I thought Mike meant what he said. But when we started having problems, we began to wonder if he'd been feeding us a line. They were the kinds of snafus he could have warned us about, so maybe he was getting revenge for the fifth-grade apple-trap trick. We didn't want to believe it, however, because he'd just been so friendly.

Trouble hit us as soon as we let the rabbits out in the yard to eat grass. We thought that all of them were as tame as Henrietta. At first they seemed to be, but after a few minutes, they started hopping away in every direction. "Let's herd them back so we can keep track of them," said Will Will.

Herding didn't work because all of the hoppers except Henrietta took off like their tails were on fire when they saw us walking toward them. They rocketed away while springing up and down like scissors snapping open and shut. Their bodies were a blur of white, gray and brown for about ten seconds before they disappeared. All that happened so fast that we couldn't believe what we'd seen.

Eventually the rabbits stopped running and settled down, but we had to spend an hour corralling them. We pulled Annabel and Betty out from beneath the back porch and found Ralph hiding in the garage behind a pile of garden tools. We finally spotted six of the smaller rabbits hopping along the road ditch in front of the house. The other five were still missing.

I was searching the front yard. Will Will had just gone back to look around the pens when he shouted, "Hey, Johnny! Those little rascals are sitting in the middle of your mom's flower bed!"

It wouldn't have been so bad if the rascals were just sitting, but they were eating, too. All of them were parked on their tails among snap dragons and zinnias. Their front legs pushed their bodies high enough so they could get mouthfuls of blossoms. Then they'd sit back and chew up what they'd bitten off.

Naturally Mom was peeved when she found out what had happened. "If those horrible beasts so much as nibble another flower, you won't have to worry about selling them. I'll skin them all alive!" she promised.

Will Will and I needed some way to keep all of the rabbits in one place when they were out eating grass. We decided to buy fifty yards of chicken wire to fence them in. We had to mow more lawns for our gradmas' friends to get money to pay for the wire. That meant we were working awfully hard to run a business that wasn't supposed to be much work at all!

"Once people start buying our rabbits, we'll be OK," said Will Will as we pounded a dozen long wooden stakes into the lawn to hold up the fence. "In about a week the eleven little guys will be ready to sell. Then we'll start hauling in the cash!"

We didn't have much time to think about money. As soon as we set up the fence, we noticed a couple of the smaller rabbits sitting back on their tails, scratching their ears with their hind feet. Soon all the rest of them were doing it, too.

"This is something Mike never mentioned," I said as I watched Betty scratching away with both back feet.

"I've got a feeling there's a lot more that Mike never told us!" growled Will Will, making a fist. "I'd like to jump on a plane to California and look him up. I'd treat him to a knuckle sandwich to show how much we appreciate what he did for us!"

"It could be worse," I replied. "At least we have Mike's book about rabbit production. Let's see what it says about itchy ears."

There was a whole chapter about what could go wrong with rabbits. We turned at least ten pages that explained mastitis, malocclusions and another dozen sicknesses we'd never heard of. Then we came across a section on ear mites.

"I'll bet that's what our rabbits have," Will Will declared. "Just listen to this: 'Ear mites are common tiny parasites. Infected rabbits will scratch their ears until they become raw and bloody. To prevent this condition, apply a liquid medication containing a mineral oil base'."

Will Will looked puzzled. "What's a 'mineral oil base' and how are we supposed to 'apply' it?"

"I haven't the foggiest idea," I said. "But we'd better find out quick!"

We called a veterinarian who said he had the medicine we needed. He told us he'd bring it to us, since he had to look at some sick cows on a farm near my house. It turned out to be a liquid we had to put into the rabbits' ears using a drip bottle.

The medicine cost ten dollars, which we borrowed from Dad. He said we could pay him back by putting away all the stuff we'd scattered in the garage when cutting the chicken wire for the rabbit fence. We got off pretty easy, however, because the vet didn't charge us for coming out. But he said we'd have to spend more money.

"Your rabbits need more vitamins and minerals," he explained. "They should be getting twice as many pellets as you're feeding them now."

"Well, old buddy, it's back to lawn-mowing," I told Will Will as he was dribbling medicine into Ralph's ears. He was having a hard time because Ralph was squirming and trying to bite.

"If it wasn't for all the loot we're going to rake in when we start selling the rabbits, I'd think about making mowing our real job," growled Will Will. "So far we've got eight old ladies who like the way we cut their grass and trim their shrubs."

"But we're working our tails off!" I complained. "Think of all those cement bird baths and plastic windmills we have to move when we cut Mrs. Burgy's grass."

Will Will had finished with Ralph and was now dropping oil into Annabel's ears. "Moving that lawn stuff isn't much worse than worrying about the next thing that's going to go wrong with our rabbit business," he insisted. " It's getting to be a king-sized pain in the butt!"

The day finally came when we were ready to sell the eleven rabbits that had been half grown when we took over Mike's business. They weren't nearly as big as Henrietta, Annabel, Betty or Ralph, but we thought they looked really good.

We'd just gotten the list of customers in the mail from Mike. It should have arrived a lot sooner, but we were sure it had all the names we needed to start hauling in money. We were ready to phone each person right away and get quick cash for the rabbits.

"Hey! Fred Flintstone buys and eats rabbits," I said, looking at the first name.

"So do Donald Duck and Mickey Mouse!" said Will Will, glancing at the next two. "I can't believe Plastic Man and Bozo the Clown are also on this list!"

It didn't take any brains to figure out that Mike had played a really dirty trick on us. Each of our "customers" was a cartoon or comic-book character. If we wanted to sell our rabbits, we'd have to start from scratch and try to get real people to buy them!

"That could take two weeks, and maybe longer!" yelled Will Will after he'd torn up the list and jumped up and down on it. "We could mow six or seven lawns by then and probably make as much money as we'd earn if we sold all eleven rabbits. By the way, what do you think they're worth?"

"That's another thing Mike should have told us," I replied. "He really hornswoggled us!"

I expected Will Will to do some more yelling, but he just smiled.

"You know, Johnny, we're really not too bad off. We've learned not to trust every varmint who says he has a good deal for us. And if we mow enough lawns, we can make all the money we need for stuff like taxidermy lessons and model airplanes."

"You're not forgetting the rabbits, are you?" I asked. "How're we going to get rid of them?"

"Why don't we just give them away? I don't think we'd have much trouble finding at least eleven kids who'd take them as pets."

"But what about Henrietta and Annabel and Betty and Ralph?" I wondered.

"We'll make Henrietta our pet and eat the other three. Mom would be glad to cook them up, and you could come over a couple of times and have dinner with us. It'd be just like the time we wolfed down that possum."

I figured rabbit wouldn't upset my stomach like possum, so I told Will Will I'd go along with that idea. "But what about all the rabbit cages and the chicken wire?" I wondered.

"We'll sell it all to Paul the Junk Man," Will Will replied. "He won't pay us much, but we won't be pressed for cash if we keep mowing lawns."

I was feeling pretty good about these plans, so I made a joke by asking what we'd do if Mike ever came back from California and wanted to know what happened to all the rabbits.

Will Will didn't laugh. Looking like he was about to chew nine-inch nails, he made two fists and snarled, "We'd pound Mike to mush, then tell him the business just wasn't right for us. I'm sure he'd get the message!"